Classroom Management

The Dance of the Dolphin

Mark Kennedy

For Brianna —

Gracious Daughter,
Graceful Mentor
In the Dance of the Dolphin

ISBN: 1-885580-17-7

TABLE OF CONTENTS

Classroom Management: The Dance of the Dolphin

Prologue

Finally, Two Weeks Off

Friday afternoon. It had finally arrived! Two weeks off. Yes, it was winter break, the thing that keeps every teacher going the first half of the school year. Of course, the problem is that I always seem to have saved four months' worth of projects to do in those two weeks, and combined with the state of exhaustion most of us are in by that point, the time off seems cruelly short.

But this vacation, my wife and I were determined to squeeze in some R&R. So it was that we found ourselves paying full price for a mere 40-minute film. The good news—it was about dolphins, a longstanding interest of mine. As the film began and we settled in, for some reason I couldn't immediately identify, one segment particularly stood out. A man who lived most of the year in the Turks and Caicos Islands had developed a relationship with a dolphin who lived a solitary existence—not unheard of, but still unusual for such communal animals. Every day the man, who we found out was named Dean, would swim out and the dolphin, JoJo, would meet him. One of their regular pastimes involved JoJo's favorite toy, which he and Dean would bat around underwater.

But it was another activity of the pair that gripped me: man and dolphin would often swim in a lazy vertical circle. Nothing profound, right? So why was I mesmerized watching that circle play out? Perhaps part of it was in thinking of the interaction and collaboration between a human being—presumably at the top of the biological pyramid—and an animal in the wild. Yet, as I watched and contemplated the juxtaposition, something deeper tugged at me.

The film went on to other things, and I forgot the scene for a moment. But later the camera returned to JoJo and Dean, in order to document a problem that arose. Dean had to leave the island for a several-months-long trip. Of course, we had to wonder how JoJo would respond, especially since it seemed the man was his only friend. This dilemma proved compelling for me. With no way of communicating his reason for being called away, Dean had no way to prepare the dolphin for his long absence. I could imagine JoJo feeling abandoned. My intention is not to anthropomorphize animals; nevertheless, the dolphin had exhibited the ability to bond with a human, as demonstrated by his showing up to play every day, which suggested to me the animal had feelings. How, then, would he feel about and react to the sudden, unexplained disappearance of his friend? I hoped it would turn out well.

Toward the end of the film, we saw the answer. We watched as Dean returned to the island and prepared to swim out to the playground which man and dolphin had shared. What would he find? As Dean arrived at the area where he and JoJo normally met, there was no sign of the animal. Although the man searched, still the dolphin was nowhere to be found. This went on for some time, and I was by no means sure JoJo would be back. But then finally he did appear. JoJo was wary, though. He refused to interact with Dean, ignoring the man's various attempts to coax him into their trademark circular dance.

Then the swimmer tried the toy. He batted it at the dolphin, hoping to get a response. But it seemed this, too, was doomed to fail. JoJo watched, but would not respond. Again, Dean persevered (how long could this guy hold his breath, anyway?). Just as I was giving up hope, the dolphin batted the toy back. From there, the old relationship seemed quickly to resume. It wasn't long before the two friends again were swimming that lazy vertical circle.

As I watched them swim, I sensed we had just witnessed something profound. I also believed it had implications for my work with students. But what were these implications? I had no idea. Through previous similar observations of nature, however, I have learned to respect such hunches, while giving the deep connections time to surface in their own manner (Kennedy 1999; 2001a). It might be awhile before I could hope to know what it meant for me and my students. On the other hand, perhaps the two weeks off might speed up the creative connections I was hoping for.

Making Connections

So although I knew it would take time, I was too intrigued just to drop the matter. Thus it was that I did spend some time trying to consciously think through what it might mean for dolphins and people to interact. Once armed with some direction in how dolphins and people—specifically adult people—relate, I hoped to go further and reach some understanding of how kids and some of those same adult people relate. Here is a synopsis of my mental journey.

As the dolphin expert Carol Howard (1995) so cogently explains, for two dolphins she worked with and studied, she and her colleagues were "aliens." Well, I can relate. At least several times during every school day, I feel my students and I are from alien planets—or at least alien environments on the same planet. Howard coined a term for this idea in the dolphin/adult-interaction arena: *coterrestrials*. It was a short step to begin to see how kids and I could be from alien worlds on the same planet, "coterrestrials" in our own right. And in fairness, I know many kids often see me the same way. This is evident in the times I'll say something which seems exceedingly profound and clever to me, and everyone—even those I can always count on to "get it"—stops and gives me that flat look.

So, if dolphins and kids are both aliens, or perhaps better, if we are alien to both of them, maybe the connections I was seeking were more than just fanciful. Maybe there were parallels to be drawn between kids and dolphins; between a classroom culture of kids and one or two adults—a community of coterrestrials—and a community of dolphins and people living as coterrestrials. Maybe it was no accident these thoughts occurred to me at the beginning of the holiday period that traditionally allows teachers to recover from the experience of running a classroom for the first half of the school year.

Well, what did I have to lose by pursuing this line of thinking? One of the central tenets of my teaching philosophy has long been that authentic interests should play a part in our schools, not just for kids but for educators, too (Kennedy 1996; Fried 2001). And something I preach daily to kids is that wrong answers are just as important as—no, *more* important than—getting the right answers. At worst, I'd have an excuse to spend a little money on some books about dolphins, which had been on my wish list for a long time (one of which turned out to be a book about this film [Cahill 2000]). At best, the search might shed some light on how to understand and explain the system of classroom management I've been using to communicate democratic and communal principles to coterrestrials for years. And if it turned out to be the latter, this might help me illuminate the system, so that others could more easily adapt it for use with their own "aliens." But to begin, I need to take you back to the week of school leading up to that holiday break.

Introduction

The Approaching Holidays

It was just days before the Christmas break andeveryone in my class was feeling the intensity of the approaching holidays. As a dangerous corollary, I found out that some of my students were involved in a he-said-she-said undertow. By the time I got word of the dispute, it had escalated through the argument stage and on to the level of threats, never idle in my county-run alternative education class where everyone is "backed up" by older homies, and violence and tragedy can be just a phone call away. I reminded myself this was not paranoia—I'd seen it happen before. And the thought of losing one more kid was more than I could take (the number of those already lost in past years was in double digits).

On the one hand, if we could get to Friday, the two weeks off would act as a natural cooling off period. On the other hand, Friday was two days away, a lifetime. I could picture it all too easily: the slowing car, the ugly flash of metal, the crack of gunshots—another tragedy erupting in a heartbeat. I'd have given *anything* for it to be Friday afternoon.

But it wasn't, and it was up to me to do something if this mess was going to be stopped. I knew from experience that calling in a harsh response—police and probation officers—would not work, would only drive the conflict out of sight. I also knew that counseling, even from trusted adults, would bring a polite but distant reaction, and would

---

Portions of this introduction were adapted from an earlier article, "Managing the Active, Differentiated-Learning Classroom," which appeared in *New Horizons for Learning Online Journal* (September–December 2001). Used with permission.

merely result in an interlude in the action. Fortunately, however, for more than a decade my classroom had been student self-governed, with the intent of nurturing educational, social, and communal authenticity through the balance of student empowerment and responsibility. To make a long story short, the current crop of student leaders was able and willing to step in and handle this situation through a combination of individual and group peer mediation. I turned them loose in an adjoining room, where they conducted a two-hour counseling/support/tough-talk session. Incredibly, when all the participants finally emerged, it became apparent that these children had gone beyond damage control, to healing; old resentments were released and old friendships between the feuding parties were reestablished. The almost-combatants were now just kids again, excited about the coming holidays, because of the work of some other kids who had earlier grown through the balance of freedom and responsibility inherent in our class management system, which we call Micro Self-Government, or just Micro.

The Dance of the Dolphin: Four Steps

Shortly after this incident, while watching JoJo and Dean swim the lazy circle, I began to see it as a dance that might be emblematic of Micro. As man and dolphin swam—or danced—the lazy vertical circle, it occurred to me they could be described as passing through four movements, or dance "steps," which could represent what I believe are the four primary ways of seeing and running classrooms (Kennedy 2001a; Hallahan and Kauffman 1994). Specifically, there are *behavioral* classrooms that put a high value on student compliance so that factual information can be efficiently disseminated. Other classrooms are *ecological* and seek conformity to societal norms in order to ensure that students will learn job and life skills. Then there are *psycho-educational* classrooms, which operate by creating an environment where learning is driven by student commitment. Finally, there are *personalistic* classrooms that seek to establish a learning community. What if all four could be combined in one classroom? In *every* one? In Chapter One we'll look more closely at each of these four classroom management views and the possibility of forming them into a circle, or dance.

A Willingness to Dance

To lead the Dance of the Dolphin and successfully use all four movements in running a classroom, the teacher, an individual with a strong predilection towards only *one* of the individual movements or steps, must be willing to admit the he doesn't know it all, that she is still learning. This will require both humility and courage on my part. Humility is needed because what I don't know and what I must learn will be seen by all. When I commit myself to the process of dancing with others, I can't always predict the exact pattern or direction that our dance will take, although I can predict the overall, or global, outcome. Entering a process which will publicly expose me to humility and risk will take some measure of courage on my part. We will talk in more depth in Chapter Two about both the requirements and benefits, personal and professional, that await the teacher willing to lead the dance.

Micro is Significant: Some Ways the Dance Works

The Dance of the Dolphin will call upon students to change, too. Essentially, it requires students to learn and practice the balance of authority and responsibility, the very foundation of democracy. As we know, in a democracy the social compact between the people and the government empowers the citizenry to make material decisions about government, including who will serve in it, but in return it requires citizens to abide by the decisions of the elected representatives. The result is our rule of law, to which even the President of the United States is obligated. For many students, this will be their first experience with having the authority to make significant decisions that affect themselves, as well as the responsibility of living with the results. Just as with the teacher, this new experience will require courage on the part of students, while paradoxically it increases the security they feel in their learning environment, an effect implicit in Maslow's work (Dickinson 2001).

Just as there are chosen leaders who make the social compact work, Micro must have leaders as well. One reason we were able to handle the situation illustrated in the opening vignette at the classroom level—in reality, the only level possible—is that students already knew that our class is not just preparation for life, but *is* life. They know that our class is not a time-out from the real world, as schooling is traditionally seen to be; we don't believe it "unprofessional" for the teacher and others to acknowledge the real-life problems they're facing; that it's OK for us all to be real people, not just academic blank slates, or talking heads with all the answers. In order for a teacher to have the freedom to let go of the traditional "command and control" mode (Fried 2001), and to follow for a while as Dean did when JoJo ascended to become the leader, she or he must have trained, encouraged, and nurtured student leaders. We will take a look at the process for doing so in Chapter Three.

Why the Dance Works: Micro Self-Government

This book is meant to combine experience with theory, to mirror a reflective practice. Therefore, it includes many suggestions and even exemplars for classroom practitioners.

There are three essentials for practicing a Micro system in the classroom: an organizational scheme, micro regulations (which replace the old list of "classroom rules"), and a micro economy. I will share samples of ways I and others have implemented each in the past, in order to flesh out the theoretical skeleton. As we shall see, however, the ultimate form these three essentials take is open to customization and revision. In fact, when teaching this concept to other teachers, I encourage them to raid my ideas and modify anything they like. More than a few of these students have far outstripped the "master." I encourage you to do the same.

Learning in the Micro Environment

Using the concepts of social compact and rule of law in the classroom and school, not merely as abstract history lessons but as tangible guidelines for classroom self-management, can have two further pragmatic benefits: Such practice reduces stress for teachers (by delegating some responsibility) and students (because they share in the authority); and, it is educationally significant, because it frees students to find and pursue the particular avenue to learning that best works for them. There are many good maps available for guiding such explorations (Sternberg 1985; Gardner 1993; Diamond and Hopson 1998; Dunn 1996). But since busy practitioners must settle on one, in Chapter Five we will call upon my own model, the idea of Learning Perspectives (Kennedy 2001a), as an example of how students can form roots and then wings in a Micro-run classroom.

This exploration will include practical suggestions for understanding and determining the natural perspective that students bring to the learning environment, for subsequently grouping them either homogeneously or heterogeneously, and for challenging them to grow into ways of thinking which at first may seem foreign to them.

From Micro to Macro: Two Success Stories

While not everyone who leaves my class has gone on to graduate *summa cum laude* from Harvard (of course, neither did I), I believe all have benefitted. Further, of the micro leaders, about 80% have stayed off drugs, have either completed high school or continued into adult school, and almost all of those have stayed in touch with me. About half are working full time to support themselves and their families, while the rest have continued into college—often at first a community college. Perhaps half of the latter have expressed interest in becoming teachers and counselors with high-risk youth. At this point, I would like to offer the changes in just two kids as an anecdotal rationale for Micro. (As always, I have mixed and matched actual events to protect identities.)

First there is Vicki, who came to my class as a sixteen-year-old child of an alcoholic father and perhaps, one suspects, a victim of sexual abuse. She was what the culture would call a "player." As is so typical, Vicki had dropped out of school in the ninth grade, and so even though age-appropriate for 11th grade, she had completed less than one full year of high school credits. In the beginning, she fell right in with the wrong people at our school, those with whom she could continue on the same course. After a few months under Micro, however, she began to become more serious about schoolwork, and at the same time seemingly more aware of others, their feelings, and their circumstances.

Vicki was by no means free from her past, though, and so it turned out she became pregnant. But even with morning sickness and doctors appointments, even with time off to have the baby, Vicki returned to school more intent and focused than ever. By doing essentially double the normal high school workload through all this, she was able to complete all her credits, pass the high school proficiency exams, and has for the past couple of years attended community college. Her goal is to work with at-risk youth, perhaps as a probation officer, social worker, or counselor.

Second, I offer Peter. Half Latino and half White, somewhat nerdy and an outcast, Peter was close to his father, but at odds with his stepmother. He had been expelled from comprehensive high school in his freshman year for dealing drugs, and had done time in juvenile hall before being released to attend a court and community school class. I always suspected Peter hid a red-hot rage behind a ready smile, although this observation was from a distance at first: Peter went through several other teachers at our school before they gave him to me—his last stop.

I sensed that it was Peter the (former?) drug dealer who first walked through my door. Yet after a few months he began to change, acting more like a stakeholder, even defending our Micro system to newer enrollees who thought it silly or childish. Within nine months, Peter became first a team leader, and then the class CEO. He held that position for another six months, until it was time for him to return to high school for his last semester so that he could graduate and walk in the graduation ceremony with his class. Peter went on to attend (and complete) an associate of arts degree and to become a full-time day manager in a regional hardware chain, a family operation known for paying well and offering excellent benefits in order to attract the best people. When he arrived the last time he came to visit me, I noticed his car was a much newer and more expensive model than mine!

There are both more and less dramatic success stories from the Micro organization structure; these two are merely illustrative. While I'm sure there are other important elements that contributed to these students' success, I'm just as sure that they would not have been able to find their own authentic, unique paths to living as independent adults and lifelong learners without the Micro experience. As an added benefit, they helped me and their fellow students become better, more enthusiastic learners and to understand through experience what the delicate dance of freedom and responsibility in a democracy is about. In Chapter Six we will look at several more such stories.

Dancing to Hope

> To speak of only one side and ignore the other is to create [skepticism] firsthand in most ordinary citizens, who know firsthand counterexamples to any single view.... Many educators in classrooms and schools feel that they have become

> pawns in the reformers' and policymakers' propaganda game that insists there is only a single best way to change the system of American schools. (Glickman 2001)

The Dance of the Dolphin provides a fuller approach than any one-sided classroom management system. It is an approach that acknowledges the complexities of human need and interaction, a more honest way to lead. And because it is honest, we will see that the Dance of the Dolphin offers hope—hope that inclusion can replace exclusion; that understanding can replace gossip and fear; that trust can suffuse distrust; that every child's natural hopefulness and exuberance can be nurtured—or rekindled—into a passion for life and lifelong learning; that every educator can be appreciated not in spite of his or her best dance step, but for it. Too idealistic? Not in my experience. But read on, and then decide whether or not you agree.

Chapter One

Man and Dolphin

The Lazy Circle of Classroom Leadership

The longer I reflected upon the lazy circular dance of dolphin and man, the more clearly I began to understand that the circle really consisted of four dance steps. Going beyond the positions in which the swimmers are shown in the diagram on the following page, we could imagine the next two positions they would swim through, thus making up the four steps of the Dance of the Dolphin. We might then correlate each step with one of the four primary goals of classroom management, first mentioned in the introduction: compliance (behaviorism), conformity (ecological management), commitment (the psycho-educational class), or community (a personal class environment). In order to better grasp these four steps, it will be important to take a look at them in table format, which we will do in Table 1-1. And in order to understand the degree to which these four views affect management in our classrooms, we will want to follow the classroom view with an examination of their importance in the field of education as a whole—and really, in society as a whole, which we will do in Table 1-2.

The linear continuum format of these tables will be followed by returning the four views to the circular dance, which we will do in Figure 1-2[1] This image will unite the four steps into the complete dance, portraying how the Dance of the Dolphin is able to encompass *all four* views of classroom management, and even of education as a whole, in a single classroom. This portrayal will intend to demonstrate how the dance is capable of meeting the primary classroom environmental needs and desires of everyone involved—children and adults. But this is only an overview of where we want to go in this chapter. Our journey must begin where for me it always begins and ends: in a single school, in a single classroom, with a single student. To get us started, I'd like for us to imagine looking in on a meeting about one student, specifically one who has not been successful in school in recent years (but of course, we don't have meetings about students who *are* having success in school).

Figure 1-1. The Dance of the Dolphin

THE GREAT DEBATE OVER CLASSROOM ENVIRONMENT

As we prepare to observe this school meeting, we need to understand that most such events—often hotly contested, as many of us who have participated in them know very well—are intertwined with the four views on classroom management that I am proposing. But perhaps even more central at this point to our understanding of the heat generated in such meetings is that we grasp the fact that the four perspectives can—and must—be grouped into two metaviews. I like to term the set of perspectives that looks for compliance and conformity, Traditionalism. The set of perspectives that seeks a classroom culture of commitment and community, I would like to call Unconventionalism. The struggle between them has been appropriately termed by some, The Great Debate (Miller 1997; *Education Week* 2000).[2]

These two metaviews have been argued for at least the past six decades. And if a debate from 60 years ago seems irrelevant, then just think of the past 60 days, because we can find just as much heat there. To illustrate this claim, we might point to several current manifestations of the tension between Traditionalism and Unconventionalism: mastery of existing knowledge vs. creation of new knowledge; conservatism vs. progressivism; knowledge transmission vs. constructivism; phonics vs. whole language; standardized testing vs. authentic assessment; building-block math instruction (mastery of one step before moving to the next) vs. exploration of math concepts; the back-to-basics movement vs. the drive for learner-centered instruction; instruction in knowledge vs. construction of knowledge. The list is almost endless.

How the Debate Shows up in the Classroom

The metaview called Traditionalism seems to me to have an undercurrent of *efficiency*. It would seem to require that the fastest route to accomplishing a task be taken, in this case the learning task. The pace of teaching (and of learning) is controlled by the teacher and extrinsic to the student (Bai 2001; Glickman 2001) in order to reach a predetermined goal in a set amount of time. The student's role in the traditional learning environment is to be responsible to "get" all the material being "taught" (spoken, handed out, or assigned) by the teacher, who acts as a "sage on the stage." All lesson planning that derives from the Madeline Hunter stepped model presupposes the Traditional learning environment, as does the current standards movement. How committed the mainstream is to this movement in the face of many challenges is illustrated by the fact that a whole issue of one of the traditionalist flagship journals was recently devoted to "Making Standards Work" (*Educational Leadership* 2001).

The metaview that I call Unconventionalism is swept along on a current of what is believed to be the most *effective* for the individual learner's growth. The pacing of learning and the motivation of students will necessarily be intrinsic to each learner. The focus of the students' role in

Table 1-1. The Great Debate Over Classroom Environment
Two Sides, Four Perspectives

	Traditionalism		Unconventionalism	
Focus of Class Time	Efficiency (Maximum Time Given to Task)		Effectiveness (Maximum Time Given to Learner's Growth)	
Student Motivation and Pacing	Extrinsic (Provided by Authority)		Intrinsic (Provided by Student)	
Citizenship Focus	Student Responsibility / Teacher Freedom		Student Freedom / Teacher Responsibility	
Teaching/Learning Perspectives	Analytic (Professor)	Normative · (Investigator)	Inventive (Innovator)	Personal (Communicator)
Goal of Class Management	Compliance	Conformity	Commitment	Community
Traditional Label	Behavioral Classroom	Ecological Classroom	Psycho-educational Classroom	Personalistic Classroom
Opponents' Stereotype	Despotic	Militaristically Uniform	Permissive	Anarchic

these classrooms will be on their freedom. Only the student will know when, whether, and how much learning has occurred; only they can determine when to slow down, stop, restart, or take an intuitive or idiosyncratic leap. The teacher will function best as a "guide on the side." Teachers who hold this metaview often detest any attempt to force them to use an efficiency model in planning for student learning (such as preparing a lesson plan that predetermines the pacing of instruction). This type of planning is not only difficult for unconventional teachers, it may in fact be impossible for them unless they are allowed, encouraged, and taught to slowly develop this ability, such as in a roots to wings model.[3]

We are now ready to further examine The Great Debate over classroom management by separating the two metaviews into four constituent perspectives. We see in Table 1-1 that there are some learners—and teachers—with an *analytic* teaching/learning perspective[4] (Kennedy 2001a), others with a *normative* outlook, some with an *inventive* perspective, and some with a *personal* view. Educators in the first category generally believe the purpose of classroom management is to get students to comply; those whose perspective is normative will focus on the conformity of students to a social norm; those with an inventive outlook will believe in establishing a mutual commitment between teacher and students; and those teachers who are more personally focused will tend to believe that the learning environment should be a community, involving both teacher and student, often in a collegial manner.

We might use a kind of shorthand for each of these views—a typology of sorts—when we refer to The Professor, The Investigator, The Innovator, and The Communicator.[5] The teacher who holds the Professor perspective and believes in compliance will view the proper classroom environment as behavioral; student compliance (that students "behave") is a must in order to transmit the maximum amount of factual information. The Communicator, in contrast, will want first and foremost to establish a classroom environment that has the feel of a community. One can easily follow the columns in Table 1-1 to see the specifics for the other outlooks. The stereotypes of each perspective's opponents are familiar to all of us in the field of education.

Back to the Meeting

But back to our meeting, which is going to show us the Great Debate in microcosm, to show us how alive and well is the argument between the two sides. In California we have something called the Student Study Team (SST) or the Student Intervention Team (SIT), which conducts a meeting to discuss a student who is having problems in school and to troubleshoot possible options for improving the situation. The SST is theoretically a place to examine the strengths and weaknesses of the student; in reality, however, such a forum is usually convened only when a teacher has just "had it" with the student.

Such is the case today. At issue is Isaac. Present at this afterschool meeting are some of Isaac's teachers: Mr. White, social studies teacher and initiator of this SST; Ms. Collins, Isaac's math teacher; and Ms. Justine, who teaches English. Also present are other "interested" parties: the assistant principal, Mr. Wolf; Isaac's mother (who, incidentally, speaks very little English); and the school counselor, Ms. Lovelace. Oh, and Isaac himself. A large drawing tablet stands open to a fresh sheet of paper on a wooden easel. Ms. Lovelace serves as facilitator for this meeting.

After introductions are made (mostly to the mother, since all the others are well acquainted, often through past conversations about Isaac), Ms. Lovelace stands at the easel with marker in hand and opens the meeting according to the SST format by asking, "What are the positive things we could say about Isaac?"

Ms. Justine says, "He's always very polite in my class." Mr. White and Ms. Collins share the thought they have previously shared out loud, *That's because you baby him, while the rest of your class runs wild.* Meanwhile, Ms. Lovelace is carefully writing the comment in bulleted fashion on the tablet.

Mr. Wolf adds, "He is not openly defiant. He always does what I tell him to do."

Ms. Collins says, "He's very bright, if he'd just apply himself," to which the facilitator replies, "Let's just stay with the positives for now," and writes *Bright*. There follows an embarrassingly long silence. Mr. White finally gives the mother a look which Ms. Justine interprets as patronizing in the extreme, and says, "Isaac's clothes are always neat and clean." Another lull follows.

"He's good at chess," says Ms. Justine.

"Oh, and he's good at sports," adds Mr. Wolf. "He just can't play because of his GPA."

Another long silence follows, and Ms. Lovelace finally says, "Let's move on to areas where Isaac could improve." She tears off the first sheet and hands it to Mr. Wolf to tape up on the wall (this way, the theory goes, everyone can see the team's list of Isaac's strengths).

Mr. White leads off with "He needs to stop disrupting my class. He speaks out of turn, and blurts out silly comments to get other students to laugh." *I probably would, too, if I had to stay awake in your class,* thinks Ms. Justine. *They don't call you the Sand Man for nothing.* Meanwhile, Ms. Lovelace is recording Mr. White's comment.

"He doesn't follow directions," adds Ms. Collins.

"He is reading when it's time to write, and writing notes when it's time to read," says Mr. White, with undisguised anger in his voice.

"Doesn't think before he acts," contributes Mr. Wolf, as Ms. Lovelace furiously tries to keep up, but still she adds, "He's often tardy."

"Asks questions about something I've just covered five minutes before," chips in Mr. White.

"Never does his homework," says Ms. Collins.

"Thinks he runs the school," asserts Mr. White. *Just like you* comes unbidden to Ms. Justine.

"Specific behaviors, please," reminds Ms. Lovelace as she writes frantically and flips to the third page of "Needed Improvements."

"Pushes class and school rules to the limit," Mr. White quickly amends.

"Has been in three fights this year," says Mr. Wolf.

"Can he even read?" asks Ms. Collins, turning to Ms. Justine. Justine begins to formulate an answer, beginning with, *He can read amazingly well when it's material in an understandable context, and which he cares about*—but the facilitator cuts this off with, "Let's stay with the agenda."

"If you give him an inch, he'll take a mile," says Mr. White. "He can't read because he's too busy talking to his friends and clowning around." This comment brings Ms. Lovelace to the end of that page on her tablet, and as she tears off the used page and hands it to Mr. Wolf, she says, "OK, let's move on to the strategies we've already used to try to help Isaac."

As Mr. Wolf mounts the fourth page of Isaac's deficits on the wall, the boy stares up, a little shell-shocked at seeing only a single page of things teachers like about him overpowered by four pages of things they don't. While a veteran of teacher disapproval, still the sheer number of negative pages dismays him. He thought they understood that when he was talking to a neighbor, he was still paying attention; in fact, he was often asking about something the teacher had said. This happened especially often in social studies, a particularly hard subject for him. He thought he had been doing something *right*, not wrong. And he had hoped that Ms. Collins would finally understand that he didn't do her homework because the way she explained it didn't make sense. He had always accepted that he was a slow learner and had no problem with her slowing down to explain things. But staying after school for "help?" They must know that just wasn't cool. He'd never live that down. In fact, he's been "jumped" by three different groups of guys already this year, calling him stupid, or accusing him of getting the whole class in trouble. No, staying after school for tutoring would just lead to more trouble, and he didn't like trouble.

In the meantime, Ms. Lovelace has labeled the new sheet, *Strategies Tried*.

"Detention," contributes Mr. White.

"Suspension," adds Mr. Wolf.

"Seating him right next to my desk," throws in Ms. Collins.

"Keeping him in at lunch to read the text along with me," says Mr. White.

"Letting him choose his own free reading book," says Ms. Justine.

"Changing his seat," says Mr. White.

"We already have something like that," says Ms. Lovelace, glad for a chance to rest her hand.

"Giving him a second chance to do uncompleted homework," says Ms. Collins.

"Assigning him an afterschool tutor—but he never comes," says Mr. Wolf.

Having filled the page, Ms. Lovelace asks, "OK, where do we go from here?" She labels a fresh sheet *Recommendations*.

"I recommend he be tested for special ed," says Mr. White.

"Put him on a strict behavioral contract," says Ms. Collins.

"Make the concepts more meaningful to him," suggests Ms. Justine.

"Well, we have to do something," says Mr. Wolf. "If the suspensions continue, he could be expelled." He directs this last statement to Isaac's mother (how much of the actual language she's followed is anyone's guess, although the tone of the voices and the number of negative sheets of paper now taped to the wall are unmistakable).

"What do you think, Isaac?" asks Ms. Collins.

"I don't know," says Isaac respectfully, although a note of resignation is detectable in his voice. "Whatever you guys decide."

Mr. White and Ms. Collins, realizing that the special education route would be a longer, time-consuming affair—and that there was really no evidence Isaac had any kind of disability anyway—quickly begin pushing for a behavior contract. When Ms. Justine questions this approach, the other two vigorously double-team her into silence. She stops her protests because she knows from experience that this meeting was really about getting Isaac onto this contract, anyway; that the views of most of the others is that Isaac has failed in his responsibility; that it was up to him to keep up with the teacher; and that if he couldn't do so, it was his responsibility to seek extra "help." After all, in the others' view, there are deadlines to meet, material to cover, standards to live up to. Justine resolves to do her best to try even harder to help him during the brief time each day when he's in her class. The actual contract is assigned to Mr. Wolf to write—he says in passing that he already has a boilerplate copy on his computer. And after the educators effusively thank Isaac's mother for coming (although no one does so by name, since they can't quite remember what it is), the meeting is adjourned by Ms. Lovelace.

Without putting too fine a point on it, I believe that we must take a moment to match the classroom environment perspective held by each of the main players in the SST meeting with those in Table 1-1. Mr. White seems to me a pretty straightforward compliance advocate. He sees the teacher's role as being the Professor, whose job it is to impart knowledge, and so he runs—and believes everyone should run—a behavioral classroom management system: there are "good" students who keep up with his lectures and assignments and should be rewarded (with grades, praise, and privileges) and "bad" students who do not, and so should be punished—like Isaac.

Next, I would say that Ms. Collins is a normative thinker, who believes that students should conform to an ecological classroom management system that will prepare them for the next "steps" in school and life: next week's textbook chapter, next year's required math course (sequenced by someone higher than she, and therefore beyond question), and the adult job market. Mr. Wolf and Ms. Lovelace don't really reveal enough about themselves for me to say with certainty which of the four perspectives they may hold, but it is fairly obvious they are traditionalists: Ms. Lovelace points to Isaac's nonconformity in his being tardy, and Mr. Wolf has a prepared contract ready to go for noncomplying, nonconforming students. Presumably, he has used it often before.

Ms. Justine is obviously one who believes student motivation and pacing must be intrinsic to be effective and students must have enough freedom to find their own route to the learning destination. For her, teacher talk, standard assignments, and one-size-fits-all textbooks do not add up to teaching, and definitely don't promote learning. I believe her thoughts on giving Isaac a choice in books demonstrate that she is seeking to further his commitment to his own learning, an unconventional and innovative approach, especially apparent when compared to White and Collins. Their shared thought that she is permissive illustrates the traditional take on her psycho-educationally managed classroom, which seeks to provide "for the needs of individuals for learning success" (Kennedy 2001a, 13).

Isaac himself is a classic personalistic learner, whose communication with others is a catalyst triggering his own learning experiences. For him, the school is an extension of the community. If Mr. White is having a bad day—if his wife is sick, or one of his children got hurt; if Mr. White got a rejection letter from a publisher on something he wrote; if Ms. Collins' car won't start in the mornings; if she is feeling overloaded with her workload—then Isaac is empathetic, ready to listen or just be there for them; ready to get some friends to look at Ms. Collins' car; ready to give up his lunch time in order to stay in and play a friendly game of chess with Mr. Wolf in order to cheer him up. Isaac cares about Mr. White, Ms. Collins, Mr. Wolf, and Ms. Lovelace, and he doesn't quite understand why they hate him so much. But he guesses it's OK: His uncle has al-

Table 1-2. The Great Debate in Education
One Goal, Two Sides, Four Perspectives

The Goal of Education: Democracy—and humanity itself—is enhanced by an equal education for everyone.

	Traditionalism		Unconventionalism	
How to Reach This Goal	Traditional, efficient, extrinsically driven classrooms. "Good" student behavior is compelled. Equal educational *opportunity*		Unconventional, effective, intrinsically driven classrooms. "Good" student behavior is impelled. Equal educational *success*	
Goal of Each Perspective	School Subjects	Life and Work Skills	Progress for People	Negotiating Life
Formal Name	Perennialism	Essentialism	Progressivism	Personalism
Representative Proponents	E. D. Hirsch Diane Ravitch	Lee Canter Gerald Anderson	Alfie Kohn Susan Ohanian	Jonathan Kozol David Elkind
Worldview	Idealism	Realism	Pragmatism	Existentialism

ready promised that when Isaac turns sixteen, he can quit school and come to work in his roofing business.

The Great Debate within the Field of Education

While the primary purpose of this book is to propose a classroom management system that will include the Isaacs of the world—as well as the educators he had problems with—it may be helpful to get above the classroom level and see how completely these strands run through the whole field of education. This will further serve to root us in reality: to demonstrate that these four classroom management perspectives and the two overarching views are real, not just unique to my own limited experience.

What Are We Really Debating?

If we are going to get above the Great Debate, if we want to turn it into the Great Synthesis so that we stop the back and forth ascendancy of one side over the other, if we want to have a complete dance so that all students and teachers—not just those who may agree with us—may become successful, passionate, and (dare we hope?) lifelong learners, then we must better understand just what we've been debating—or refusing to debate.

As we see in Table 1-2, the debate at the higher level begins with a seeming agreement: *Democracy—and humanity itself—is furthered by an equal education for all.* This "agreement" immediately breaks down, however, because the term *equal* has different connotations for the two sides. To traditionalists, which Sleeter (1996) calls the dominant position (by which she means gender, ethnic and socio-economic dominance, but which I am adapting to include the dominance of the whole modern period of history), society is fair and open to all, and those who don't succeed in society's preparation for life (schooling) "lack ambition, effort ... etc." For those interested in following this further, an eloquent counter to Sleeter's view is that of Shelby Steele (1988).

But for our purposes, let's complete Sleeter's image. To those not born to the traditional inside track necessary for economic and academic success in Sleeter's scheme, the alternative or minority position, which would certainly describe unconventionalism in the field of education today, holds that society is "unfair and rigged." Further, those who don't achieve "success" in this system are not losers as mainstream society would say, but "strong (and) resourceful" (Sleeter 1996, 120). This appears in alternative ways, as illustrated by Isaac's plan to work with his uncle. Steele, on the other hand, would be a proponent of the traditional view, believing that everyone has equal access to success in school, but that every individual is responsible for making the most of it.

To sum up our discussion of the Great Debate: Traditional educators believe that through strategically planning "equal" (standard) student curriculum and instruction, each student has an equal opportunity to be successful in school. Traditionally managed classrooms and instructional "delivery models" are seen as the most efficient way to ensure such equality. In contrast, unconventionalists see equal educational opportunity as providing what is specifically necessary for each individual student's learning, in other words, what is effective. Leveling the field made unlevel due to huge differences in resources that tilt the playing field so that "equal opportunity" for these students is anything but equal, is actually an uphill battle.

We see further in Table 1-2 that the difference in the understanding of "equal" is simply the Great Debate on a different level. So, the familiar split between the traditional and the unconventional camps continues. Just as in the classroom version, the former is often an effort to attain the highest *efficiency* in the learning endeavor, while the latter is more often a drive for *effectiveness* (Drucker [1993] makes this same point in the corporate realm). Further, the traditional learning setting relies on extrinsic motivation for students (Bai 2001; Glickman 2001), which is determined by adult authority and which requires a heavy dose of student responsibility.

But the traditional philosophy can also be profitably further distinguished into its own two camps: perennialism and essentialism. Lee and Marlene Canter's (1976) assertive discipline system of rewards and punishments is perhaps the most famous illustration of the essentialist view. This perspective believes education should be functionally realistic, as in making students ready to *function* in a capitalist economy. High stakes testing, or the student accountability movement, is a manifestation of the perrenialistic view that there is an ideal body of knowledge to be learned. Such a belief has fostered lists of items every child "should know" (e.g., Hirsch 1996) and a scorn for the "progressive reforms" of the past 100 years (Ravitch 2000). The actual implementation of the ideal learning form would necessarily include testing for mastery of that ideal, which is exemplified in the current push for national standards, testing, and alignment of curriculum and tests—often with the aid of Total Quality Management principles, such as the recently highly-touted effort of Gerald Anderson in the Houston School District (Barlow 1999).

In contrast, the unconventional school/classroom setting runs more on intrinsic student motivation (Glickman 2001), which enhances student freedom and results in creativity and construction of meaning. Like the traditionalist metaview, unconventionalism can be further parsed into two subviews: progressivism and personalism. A progressive, forward-looking educational perspective engenders student learning by engaging them in issues that are real today. It challenges students—and educators—to think in new directions, to try forward-looking inventive solutions. This view is evidenced in the writings of Alfie Kohn (1996; 2000) and Susan Ohanian (2001). Rounding out the unconventional proponents of the Great Debate in the current forum are more personalistic, some might say humanistic or even existential proponents of education, such as Jonathan Kozol (1991) and David Elkind (1995). For them, the entire experience of every student is central to their educational experience; school is not/cannot be compartmentalized from life outside school. In short, a student's experiences outside of the school walls and inside the school walls are of a single piece, and any attempt to reduce them to separate components in a child's life is unhealthy and even dangerous to children.

Why the Great Debate is Too Expensive to Continue

There are two huge costs to the Great Debate in education, either of which by itself should give us pause, but which together act synergistically to do mammoth harm. The first cost is that since there is never a clear "winner," the debate never stops. This might be thought of as a pendulum swinging back and forth between Traditionalism and Unconventionalism every ten to fifteen years. One side holds dominance and persecutes the other for a decade or so. And then the dominance swings. As a reminder of the earlier examples, we might think recently of the ascendency of whole language through perhaps the mid-90s. But then, as pendulums do, this one began to swing back so that now the term "whole language" is not spoken in polite company; phonics is the new monarch in this subfield. The field of math reveals a similar pattern (Reys 2001). But, alas, whatever currently reigns, it will end and the pendulum will swing again—unless we become just a little wiser and prevent this from happening.

The second cost is inherent in the first: These ten- to fifteen-year swings from one approach to the other take up roughly the entire K-12 educational experience of a child. So, if a child enters kindergarten under a phonics regime, she will have no choice but to attempt to learn language through a phonics system. If she happens to be an unconventional learner, her whole life may be altered irrevocably. Perhaps more to the point of classroom management, if this same kindergartner is not a traditional learner—if she enters school needing to see personal significance, to participate in a community of learners, to see how it ties to her experience with others in the classroom and her experience outside of school—then she will likely be at risk of failure for the next thirteen years. By becoming perennially entangled in the Great Debate, we are doing this very thing to children.

Somewhat ironically, it was John Dewey, revered icon of progressivism, who first drew my attention to the problem inherent in taking an either/or position in education, in forcing a choice between *either* a traditional approach *or* his own progressive approach:

> I have suggested ... that those who are looking ahead to a new movement in education ... should think in terms of Education itself rather than in terms of some "ism" about education, even such an "ism" as "progressivism." For in spite of itself, any such movement that thinks and acts in terms of an "ism" becomes so involved in reaction against other 'isms' that it is unwittingly controlled by them. (1963, 6)

I don't believe Dewey really meant for us to throw out the suffix "ism," which merely connotes any ideology. He just meant for us to embrace perspectives that are inclusive rather than exclusive. For example, holism means whole-ism, the whole and not a mere fragment of the truth, as in a simple one-sided reaction against fragment-ism, or as we sometimes call it, reductionism. Dewey's contemporary, Dorothy Sayers (1987), made the same point in the broader philosophical context, saying that it is the tension of a bridge that gives it value, that without both sides there is no bridge to cross at all.

Glickman calls this battle one of "ideological absolutes" and, with Dewey, admonishes us that "Ultimately, an American education must stand on a foundation that is wider than the beliefs of any one individual or any one group" (2001, 147). I would add, not just an American education but any *just* education, whatever the geopolitical landscape.

Figure 1-2
The Dance of the Dolphin
Classroom Leadership that Encompasses Traditionalism (Student Responsibility, Teacher Freedom) and Unconventionalism (Student Freedom, Teacher Responsibility)

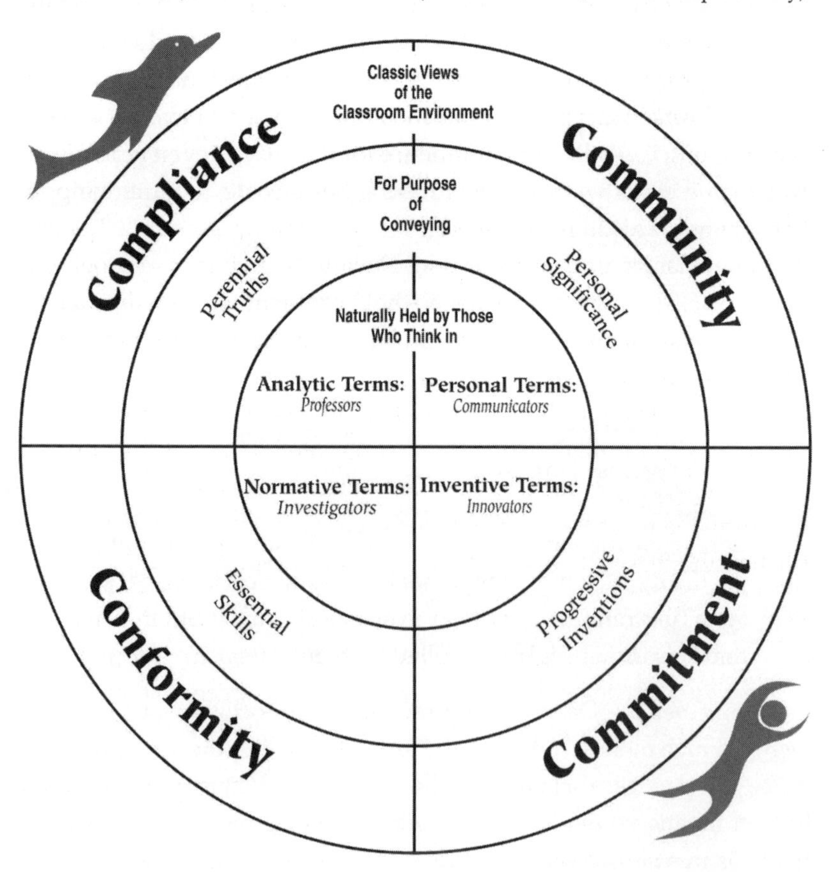

Two Pseudo-Solutions to the Great Debate in Education

In a vein similar to Glickman, Brandt calls for the "intentional differentiation of schooling" (2001, 153), by which he means sorting people into schools or classrooms of like-minded individuals. This is probably fine in some homogeneous geographical and socio-economic locales, but it is not in the urban centers that are home to so many of our children. Those of us who actually work in those schools and classrooms know that reality does not often lend itself to this task of dividing people so neatly. Persons of different outlooks are going to end up in one school, and probably very often, even in one classroom—just as they do now. However, I submit that if we can't make democracy work within our classrooms, then we can't make it work outside of them. We can't turn democracy on and off at will. And if we can't make democracy work in a classroom, we aren't making it work as a school, a school district, a county or state, a nation, or as a people. A democracy fails if it has pockets of tyranny, whether it's the tyranny of a traditional top-down view, or the tyranny of an unconventional student-centered view; if one or the other is forced on someone of another view, it is tyranny.

A second pseudo-solution is a rationalization of Traditionalism. If Mr. White were reading this, he would probably be thinking, "I do this already; I let students collaborate." But actually I believe he is really saying, "I command their collaboration: my way, on my timetable, by my rules, to get my (right) answer." Such a scenario is still a form of compliance, not an openness to commitment or community. The test must be: How willing am I as a traditional teacher to welcome student-suggested solutions that are totally new to me? How willing am I to treat students collegially? How open am I to hearing and implementing student suggestions to changing how we do business? So while Mr. White probably thinks he already has times of collaborative learning in his classroom, in reality he is acting out his side of the Great Debate. And in the case of Isaac, White and his co-traditionalists "won."

The Dance of the Dolphin: Resolving the Great Debate in the Classroom

I have demonstrated the importance of seeing and including all four distinct classroom management steps, or movements, in the Dance of the

Dolphin. Still I would like to highlight this approach with another analogy, a simpler one. Many sporting games are composed of four quarters. Two come readily to mind: American/Canadian football, and basketball. Obviously, each quarter is essential; to suggest omitting the third quarter of a football game, for example, would certainly be strange. To begin with the second quarter of a basketball game, to end with the third quarter of a football game, would obviously distort our entire view of the game. To omit a quarter would obviously preclude any match from being a whole. Just so, to omit any of the four steps of the Dance of the Dolphin, would change the entire connotation of the term "dance," which implies *whole* dance. And we will need the whole Dance of the Dolphin if it is to improve the way our classrooms are run, our classroom cultures, and education itself.

Indeed, we will need to use all four steps in the same classroom. As a classroom teacher, I will want compliance at certain times. This can be illustrated by an example from the larger society: I live on a modest suburban street where there are many small children. The street, however, gets used often as a thoroughfare when the real thoroughfare, which parallels it, is busy. Even though the speed limit is 25 mph, cars routinely go 45 or 50, and sometimes even more. This happens even though kids' play often spills over into the street. I have had many near misses when slowing to turn into my driveway, especially when children may be occupying it and an impatient driver speeds around me—often miscalculating which way I will turn and his own speed, and not seeing the children at all. In this situation compliance of all drivers with the speed limit is essential.

This analogy has direct application for the classroom. There will be times when I will want and need student compliance. For example, during traditional teaching times when I may be leading a discussion or lecturing to impart perennial truths in the traditional, professorial manner, I will want students to be essentially in a traditional learning mode: quiet, attentive, and receptive to my direct teaching.

On the other hand, when in my own self-contained classroom, for example, I always make sure that such intensive times of teacher-imparted knowledge are followed by unconventional classroom environment times, so that students have time to collaborate and/or commune with each other or even their own spiritual and emotional side/self. Traditional learners will often use this time after a traditional teaching session to organize the information so that it can be retrieved more efficiently. Unconventional learners, however, will need such times to process the information. That is, they have not yet learned it by the time I have finished talking, but they will actually learn it in community with other students, or even with me as I switch roles to colleague, and for some, as they use the information to understand its impact—or potential impact—on their own world.

Even during these unconventional times, however, I may return to remind students of issues of compliance or conformity. They will need to comply with the standard class and school safety rules. And I may ask them to conform to my expectations for such collaborative learning times. For example, I may ask them to speak to each other as if they are in a library: 25 to 35 voices at normal conversational level can easily create so much chaos that I can't even hear the person seated right next to me.

This simple illustration of the blending of the four steps of the Dance of the Dolphin shows how the adroit management of a single classroom can make learning equal and accessible for all learners. The dance is so simple that we might misconstrue its simplicity as unimportant, or even already in place. Neither is the case. While it is not difficult, neither is it automatic or something we can take for granted or brush aside.

Conclusion

As I sit back after writing this and reflect upon the lazy circular dance of dolphin and man, the importance of the four distinct steps, or movements, and how each is essential to the complete dance, seems clear. In later chapters, we will explore ways the dance can slide from step to step at different times and in different situations. But for now we can understand how these four steps can work together to provide a path to the ideal held by each side in the Great Debate: That an equal education for all furthers democracy—and humanity itself. But the first question we must answer if the Dance of the Dolphin is to become reality is, "How is it possible to get outside one's own favorite dance step and do the whole dance?" I believe I can show not only how it is possible, but that it is pleasantly rewarding. But this will challenge us to get beyond the either/or of old-style versus new-style classroom management. I call this the Classroom Leadership Challenge, which we will take up in Chapter Two.

Notes

1. Young (2001) recently reminded us this was called by the ancient Greeks "squaring the circle," and that "bringing the process back into the community might be described 'circling the square,' ... in essence (creating) sacred space," because of the mathematical, rational impossibility of the task. I think the Dance of the Dolphin done well in a classroom creates such sacred space, larger and more sanctified than simply the sum of the parts (teacher, students, four walls).

2. Both Miller and *Education Week* call the two sides Traditionalism and Progressivism. For reasons that will become clear as we further parse the two metaviews into the four subviews, I prefer not to use Progressivism to represent the second metaview.

3. I introduced my take on this concept in Chapter Four of *Lessons from the Hawk* (Kennedy 2001a) as a way to nurture students, beginning from their natural inclinations and growing into those that are less natural: from weaknesses to wings.

4. When just speaking of students, these are termed Learning Perspectives; when adding in educators, who also have a primary perspective, I prefer to call them Teaching/Learning Perspectives.

5. In *Lessons from the Hawk* (Kennedy 2001a), where these were first set out, I called them Professor, Scientist, Inventor, and Guide. The first three were borrowed from Garmston and Wellman (1992).

Reality Checks

1. What is your dominant view of classroom management? Think back to a disagreement that you have had with a student, colleague, boss, or family member. What was *their* dominant perspective? Do you think that a difference in natural expectations might have played any part in the confrontation?

2. Write down the names of two or three students who "get under your skin," or whom you just haven't been able to connect with. What perspective on classroom management do you think they bring to your class? Is this perspective the same as yours? Is it even on the same side of the Great Debate? What could you do to bridge the difference?

3. Write out your recollection of a meeting similar to Isaac's SST. Identify the undercurrents of the Great Debate that were running just under the surface.

4. Share your anecdote from the previous reality check with a friend, a college class, or a small group of colleagues. How do they see the Great Debate playing out?

5. Rewrite the same story so that all participants were aware of and open to the Dance of the Dolphin.

Chapter Two

Leading the Dance

The Leadership Challenge

As I pulled the mail from the box one afternoon, I caught a glimpse of the cover of a highly respected educational journal and saw that the issue's theme was "The Leadership Challenge." I was pretty sure before even getting it into the house that I knew that the journal's editors and contributors meant the daily realities facing site, district, and state administrators. But being a classroom teacher and not much occupied with the challenges of these upper-echelon positions, my take was wholly different: I thought of the challenge of *classroom* leadership.

While this may seem a straightforward concept and not really worthy of much discussion, the connotation I have in mind is somewhat richer. To understand why I say this, we only need remember that one of the traditional icons of teacher training/evaluation for the past 150 years has been classroom *management*. As used by most educators in my experience, this means the degree of direct control the teacher has of her classroom, as well as her grasp of various techniques for gaining and maintaining such a milieu of control:

> Classroom management has always been an important skill for teachers.... That term, however, [has connoted] a top-down organization which has rapidly lost favor in recent years.... It is important of course to make sure students are "on task" in a fairly orderly environment in which they help establish their own rules, take responsibility for their own be-

---

Parts of this chapter first appeared in the article "Where Do We Go From Here? September 11 and Jury Duty" (Kennedy 2001e).

> havior, and are strongly motivated to learn [in which case] they do not need a manager. (*New Horizons for Learning* 2001)

This view of the need for *both* order *and* student self-determination echoes the effect that the Dance of the Dolphin can have in moving us beyond the either/or of the Great Debate in classroom management. While the term "classroom management" is useful, I like to broaden it by including a sense of classroom leadership, so that we understand that the classroom environment will at times be traditional and at times, unconventional.

Successful classroom leadership, in my opinion, is based on a teacher's skill in leading the Dance of the Dolphin. Such leadership will be more challenging in practice than merely understanding of the concept on paper. We will cross the gap from the safety of the two dimensional to the messiness of the three dimensional. We will be attempting to lead students through all four steps of the dance even when we don't yet have all the answers; that is, we will have to give ourselves over to the dynamic process of actually dancing, often having to intuit and sense, rather than reason and plan, in leading with the step that at the time seems most appropriate.

If education is to improve in ways healthy for kids; if we are to reach the Isaacs and other high risk students in our classrooms, then we must accept the leadership challenge. We must be willing to move beyond choosing *either* the adult-centered, control model of classroom management, *or* the student-centered, collegial classroom environment, and be willing to accept the challenge of becoming leaders who know when and how to use both. To do this well, we will first need to learn the rhythm of the dance.

Getting the Rhythm

We saw in Chapter One how the solitary dance of Traditionalism, whether focused on the specific step of behaviorism with its one-view expectation of student compliance, or ecologicalism with its one-view assumption of student conformity, hurt Isaac's chances to do well in school—and we all know too many Isaacs. We noted in Chapter One that if an educator's natural step is compliance—if that is his dominant need in running the classroom—then this must be balanced with the complementary step of commitment: that his expectation for student compliance must be matched in equal or greater degree with his commitment to the student.

I would like to draw out this concept with the help of Figure 2-1. We see in the graphic that the coterrestrial, represented by the dolphin, is positioned at the compliance step. We could follow the rhythm of the dance by beginning at this step, which I have labeled "1" for the sake of clarity. We would then begin the dance this way: As the coterrestrial (student/ subordinate), *I comply,* but this is *so that* as the teacher (or other adult educator/superordinate), as represented by the swimmer, *you commit*—to my needs. If we are calling this step one[1] of the dance, then we see in Figure 2-1 that step two would go like this: *I commit* (as the superordinate) to your welfare, *so that you comply* (as the subordinate) to my requirements.

Figure 2-1
The Dance of the Dolphin
Leading/Following/Leading/Following
Traditionalism Unconventionalism

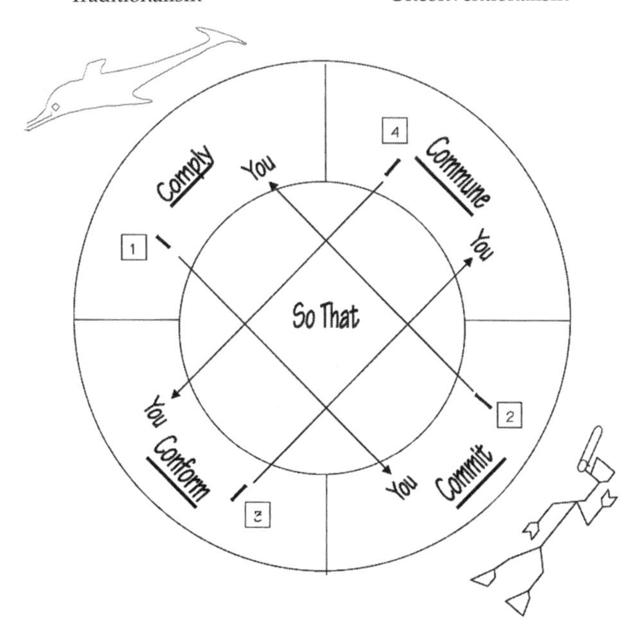

Step three could be understood, in this case beginning from a coterrestrial vantage point, as *I conform* to your vision of societal (beginning with this very classroom) norms, *so that you sometimes will commune* with me—will see me as a colleague at times. And in step four, the superordinate says *I* want to *commune* with you *so that* I can later ask that *you conform* to the norms which I believe you will need to be happy, safe and productive in my organization—and life.

Teacher Professionalism And the Great Debate

Just as in Chapter One we inserted analytical tables between the more holistic circular figures, I think we might profit by stretching Figure 2-1 into the linear, tabular format of Table 2-1. The purpose for this is to lay to rest any objections that these ideas are unprofessional for teachers, and therefore not legitimate. The table will seek to point out that such a view is actually merely more of the same Great Debate. Unless and until we can clear away some of the presuppositions held by each side, we cannot proceed with the degree of understanding and honesty we will need to break through to the Dance of the Dolphin in our classrooms and schools.

We see in Table 2-1 that traditionalists in this area view teaching as a profession. There often follows a lengthy list of what it means to be professional (which I have attempted to summarize), such as a distance kept from students, since subordinates must respect the position regardless of the person who holds it. Further, students must earn a teacher's approval through their work product—what they *do*—and their compliant and conforming behavior—again, what they do. The Traditionalist sees the outward form of the teacher taken together as a significant indicator of professionalism: how formally one dresses, timeliness, organization, fitting in to the normal behavior expected by society, and requiring students to do the same.

On the other hand, Unconventionalists see education as a calling and desire respect for their personal traits, their commitment to student success, and for the community which they establish so that students can achieve their success in a warm, safe environment. These unconventionalists inherently approve of students just for being human—for who they *are*, and not conditionally, based on academic or behavioral performance.

We see this debate played out in conflicts every day in school hallways, in teacher lounges, and in teacher education courses in which the

Table 2-1. Teacher Professionalism
The Primary Views

	Traditionalism		Unconventionalism	
Teaching is seen as a	Profession		Calling (Vocation)	
Teacher expects	Respect for the position held regardless of the particular person		Respect for the person in the position, notably disregarding differences in position	
View of Students:	Students must earn teacher's approval		Students inherently have teacher's approval	
Teaching is about	*What* we teach, and what those we teach become. What teachers and students *do*.		*Who* we teach, and who those we teach become. Who teachers and students *are*.	
Professionalism is	Teacher dress, timeliness, organization (*Form*)	Normative Societal (*Function*)	Focus on *future* shared by teacher and students	Networking to consensually negotiate *fullness* in life
Professional evaluation should judge	Compliance to form	Conformity to function	Commitment to student success	Community established by the teacher

professor holds one view and some students another; among teacher educators themselves and, of course, in the news media and the political arena. We could write a whole book on these larger examples of the debate over whether teaching is a profession or a calling, but that is not my purpose—or passion. Rather, my passion is that every child retain—right through 12th grade—the natural excitement for learning, the natural curiosity and wonder about everything there is to know that we see in toddlers.

> If we see a child who is two or three, perhaps four years old, we find a free human. Why is this human free? Because this human does whatever he or she wants to do. The human is completely wild. Just like a flower, a tree, or an animal that has not been domesticated—wild! And if we observe humans who are two years old, we find that most of the time these humans have a big smile on their face and they're having fun. They are exploring the world. They are not afraid to play. They are afraid when they are hurt, when they are hungry, when some of their needs are not met, but they don't worry about the past, don't care about the future, and only live in the present moment. (Ruiz 1997, 102-103)

The Teacher as Leader/Follower

To achieve the necessary clarity which we will need to make schooling a continuation of the love for learning and life built into every young child, I believe we need to avoid imposing our side of the Great Debate on kids. We need to learn what all true leaders know, including Dean the swimmer: The leader will sometimes be in the ascendant position as a traditional leader, and sometimes in the descendent position, as would a traditional follower—or, an unconventional leader. This is the classroom leadership challenge.

In trying to explain my vision and practice of classroom leadership through the Dance of the Dolphin, you will see that I don't pretend to have all the answers, but only to be on the journey, the path, toward understanding and becoming a leader/follower. This journey has led me to identify ten characteristics which I believe must be exhibited and modeled by the exemplary teacher leader/follower:

- respect for authority (especially important to steps one and three);
- peace with colleagues (equally applicable to all four steps);
- teaching understanding and empathy, dialogue and compromise in order to reach consensus (two and four);
- contentment with what one has, at least for today, instead of striving for that which is always just out of reach (one, two and four);
- nurturing courage and hope in students (two and four);
- exhibiting patience, patience, and more patience (four);
- drawing healthy boundaries for kids (one and three);
- protecting the natural enthusiasm of youth (one and two);
- taking the time, maturity, and understanding to listen to, learn from, and follow students (three and four); and
- acting according to our most deeply held beliefs (all steps).

It might be important to understand and acknowledge at this point an aphorism that has guided my journey. I have encountered this truth in many different places and at many different times, and so have taken the liberty of synthesizing it as my own prerequisite for becoming a classroom leader. It is this: *I can't keep what I don't give away, and I can't give away what I don't have*. This is obviously not true in the material world. In fact, just the opposite is true: With material wealth, I can only keep what I don't give away, and if I give it way, I don't have it any longer. Any material understanding of the principle is laid to rest by this ancient Shaolin admonition: "Amass a store of gold and jade and no one can protect it. Claim wealth and titles and disaster will follow." So, I can't keep what I don't give away. At the same time, it is impossible to give what I don't have myself. If, then, I must give it away to keep it, and if I must have it to give it away, then it cannot be material. It must be immaterial, or what we might call spiritual.

If you are not accustomed to, or even comfortable with, speaking about the spiritual, please don't be put off by my doing so here. I am not some mystic about to take you on an impractical tangent. Rather, I'm a classroom teacher, who spends his days dealing with kids who are coming down with a cold or the flu, who may have had an argument with a parent on the way to school, who are concerned about getting enough to eat for lunch, who may be from families so poor that the kids don't have coats to wear to school in the winter. My day-to-day world is as pragmatic as it gets. But, perhaps ironically, finding ways to meet those pragmatic challenges, another of which is including every child in the learning process and the classroom environment, has led me to the realm of the spiritual.

Another caveat which I would like to add is that, by "spiritual" I certainly don't mean religious, and even less do I mean any particular religious tradition, although for some readers, that may be an important part of *their* spirituality (Miller 2001, 34). Rather, I mean that each of us, when we were "free humans" years ago, had a definite, distinctive spirit—and probably for those around us then, as for the toddlers we see today, it was easy to spot! So when I say spiritual, I mean reconnecting with that which is a natural part of all of us, our spirit. It is also important to see that if we all have spirits (just as we all have bodies), then the spiritual part of us cannot be ignored, even though the modern world may teach us to do so. We can easily see that all human beings are connected physically, are all flesh and blood, are all related materially; I only mean to remind us that we are also alike in that we are also spiritual beings, and must allow ourselves to become reacquainted with this aspect of ourselves and others if we are to grow in ways that will allow us to become classroom leaders—to do the Dance of the Dolphin well.

So, the guiding truth for the journey I have undertaken to identify the prerequisites for a classroom leader is mostly from the realm of the spiritual, where it is certainly true that *however* much I give, I will get back even more. Mother Teresa's life was a testament to this truth—why else would she give away funds that accompanied the Nobel Prize? The prerequisite for learning the Dance of the Dolphin, then, may be summarized as follows: what I want for myself, I must want even more for others.

Respect for Authority

By respect for those in authority, I certainly don't mean blindly trusting in their infallibility. I mean respecting the position, the responsibility that the position entails, and the authority that issues from taking that responsibility. I know this is a somewhat idealistic and some would say archaic (even reactionary) view of the very human people who serve in positions of authority. It certainly doesn't come easily to me. But I believe it is essential for becoming a classroom leader/follower.

If a teacher is at odds with the site administration or anyone else in the chain of command, kids will pay the price. We might be able to understand this better through the use of the analogy of a family.[2] The familial analogy might apply, for example, if a kid's parents are at odds with her grandparents. In this situation, which many of us have experienced in one role or another, a sense of unease settles on the child because of the questions it raises. Who is right? To whom should loyalty go? Or the child may wonder, should I be divided? Whose side do I take in an outright confrontation? If one side wins, what are the effects on the losing side? How would I feel about that? Must I sacrifice the love, approval, and acceptance of one side or the other? This is exactly the position in which we place kids when we indulge in the Great Debate in our schools.

This situation can go from the covert to the overt if one of the sides tries to get at the other through the child (sometimes called triangulation [Lerner 1989]). We all know of child custody cases that are more about adults "winning" than what's best for children. And we have all probably experienced this in the professional realm when one teacher spends class time putting down a colleague and maybe even trying to win kids to his side. "Thoughts are like arrows: Once released, they strike their mark. Guard them well or one day you may be your own victim" (Navajo entry in Zona 1994, 20).

In fact, I think of a time when I witnessed this in a school. The teacher (parent, in our analogy), Ms. Smith, was fairly permissive; the administrator (grandparent), Mr. Whitmore, more authoritarian. This was especially evident in the expectations for and the way each treated a particular student, William. This difference led to conflicts which played out both in private and in public, and eventually to censure for the teacher. The child tried to please both sides, which left him to try to act one way around the teacher, and another around the administrator. But at all other times, William just acted like himself, a smart, happy-go-lucky kid with a sharp wit and a lazy streak. He would often be this way, for example, in elective classes, where militantly traditional teachers would promptly complain about him to the office—Mr. Whitmore—and Ms. Smith would again be called on the carpet for her permissiveness, which presumably caused William to think he could act "this way" whenever he wanted.

My point is not to justify weak or callous administrators. Rather, it's that Mr. Whitmore, faults and all, still held the position of being responsible for the entire school site, and not just Ms. Smith's classes. It's important to remember that the Dance of the Dolphin includes traditional steps, too. So let us recognize two things: Whitmore had the headaches of every problem in the school (so any one person's needs could not be the center of his attention) and William was the one who really paid for the ongoing disagreement between these two adults. If we adopt this principle of respect for authority, we may take some heat over not battling administrators over everything we disagree with.

After watching this melodrama unfold over a period of about two years, some three years later I happened onto the 16-year-old William—and barely recognized him—in fact, I didn't recognize him; he recognized me. This was partly because he had grown, but much more because he was sporting full gang regalia: from the bandana wrapped over and tied around the top of his shaved head, to the white undershirt worn in 50-degree weather, and the size 56 khakis on a 29-inch waist, cut off below the knees, into which knee-length white socks disappeared. Even I, his friend, was scared to think what might reside in those deep pockets and many folds. How much the experience of being squeezed between the myopia of Smith and Whitmore contributed to this situation could well be debated, but it seemed clear to me as I looked at him and saw tragedy in his future that he was not helped by the "family" disagreement in which he was the pawn. Ms. Smith would have done him more good by finding some kind of balance with Mr. Whitmore, however distasteful it may have been for her. Instead, both adults ended up as victims, by losing the child each purported to be so passionately concerned about.

Peace with Colleagues

On the heels of respect for authority is peace with colleagues. Just as a child is forced to choose sides (or, they are chosen for her) in a vertical dysfunction, so horizontal strife among colleagues, teacher and parents, or support staff, is unsettling and anxiety producing for students. If a student's parent and teacher disagree without resolution, then who does the student listen to and obey? Or, if a student's third and forth period teachers, who are tasked to teach a two-period core section together, have a running feud, each daily talking the other down to the students, will this help or hurt the child's ability to learn? This is akin to having parents do the same thing: To whom does the child give allegiance? What then happens between the child and the other parent?

For example, let's say I don't view enforcement of the school rules the same way a colleague does. A kid is seen doing something she shouldn't on the way to school, by both of us as we drive by—maybe smoking and wearing something way out of dress code. By the time she arrives on campus, there is no sign of cigarettes and she is suddenly in dress code. In applying the door-to-door responsibility rule of the school for the child, my colleague insists to the Dean of Discipline the student be punished. I see his point, but this is counterbalanced by all the time I have spent over the last semester working with her and her parents just to get her to come to school at all and not to run away from home yet again.

This difference in perspective between my colleague and me can turn ugly if we become entrenched in our positions. This ugliness can easily turn into a way of life, becoming a multi-year feud over whether compliance to rules (dance step one) or commitment to school (step two) is the higher priority. Not being at peace with colleagues and/or the administration makes us preoccupied with self-justification, reliving our last interaction, plotting our next one. And this steals us away from being emotionally present for students in the moment and even mentally unavailable.

In reality, we saw in Chapter One that we must have both compliance and commitment for effective classroom leadership. I must also be willing to find common ground with my colleague, to find collegiality. This is for me, for him, but also for the student and parent—for all of us who win or lose together.

Modeling Empathy and Consensus

I can't begin to count the number of times I've heard teachers in the staff lounge, inservice presentations, or even college classes say, "I'm not there to be a student's friend; I'm their teacher." Or, "I don't get involved with students' problems; I'm a professional." But I would point back to Table 2-1, and say that being a good classroom leader doesn't require a "professionalism" that makes us less human, to be callous to a child experiencing pain. I believe professionalism is not about wearing a tie or skirt to work. Nor is "professionalism" adequate cover to hide being cold, mean-spirited, or unhelpful to students, colleagues, or parents. If some of the most significant lessons kids learn—as measured by what they remember for life—are caught in teachable moments, instead of taught in prepared lesson plans, then empathy is infinitely more professional than how I dress or whether I plan curriculum days, weeks, or months in advance, in multi-step lessons without regard for what students may be feeling or needing on any of those particular future dates. In other words, traditional views of professionalism must be balanced with unconventional concerns for collegiality and shared outcomes. This is merely another example of the dynamics of Figure 2-1, of the necessity of the whole Dance of the Dolphin.

Similarly, if accepting and approving of others, especially those who see things differently from us, models and extends empathy, consensus is merely another avenue in the effort to understand and include. Instead of making top-down, bossy decisions, consensus requires all involved to agree. But this won't be easy. We are not well-suited to consensus in the Western world. Let me explain.

What usually passes for consensus in education in my experience is the policy makers and bosses (*Deciders* and *Tellers* in Kennedy 2001a, Chapter 6) browbeating subordinates into accepting the boss's position, perhaps with very slight concessions to dissenting subordinates (I have seen some extremely suave browbeaters at work, but nonetheless, the animal is what it is). This shortcut to "shared decision making" can certainly not be called consensus. Even democracy is not consensus. Democracy, wherein a vote is held and the majority rules, can be a blunt instrument used by 51% to bludgeon the 49%[3] into doing something they disagree with. Pragmatically, a false consensus directly harms those forced to compromise; and in turn, indirectly harms the whole enterprise, including the very boss who pushed so hard to get his own way. Thank goodness we don't define consensual sex as one side—perhaps 51% of the total body mass—arm twisting the other into submission.

Instead, we might profit from linking the concept of consensus to the word *concentric*, meaning to have a common center. The goal of working toward consensus is for everyone involved, through a process of interaction with one another, eventually to occupy a place equidistant to a commonly agreed upon center. No one person (point on the circle) has any more or less voice—or even preunderstanding—in determining what the common center ultimately will be. Rather, all are responsible for and empowered to search out that common center point. In my experience, it will always turn out to be much different from what most of the participants—and especially the boss—envisioned when beginning.

Let me suggest an analogy to illustrate how the lack of empathy, compromise, and consensus can harm the entire organization. When a construction crew prepares the cement for the foundation of a house, it must be sure to properly mix the ingredients of the cement: sand, water, and the cement mix itself. If not done thoroughly, perhaps some pockets of sand, and other pockets of water will remain under the veneer of concrete. But later, when the builder has moved on to another phase of construction, perhaps as the crew attempts to build on this veneer, one of the workers steps on a thin layer which crumbles into the unmixed pocket underneath. Of course, now the problem is more than just this one spot; the whole foundation must be suspect. The entire building is compromised.

Likewise, forcing agreement to a so-called consensus session leaves the weak pockets unmixed, under a thin veneer of agreement. The veneer will in all likelihood later crumble under the slightest pressure. If we want students to take responsibility for their learning and classroom environment; if we want parents to share in decisions and responsibility; if we want to move a school site, district, state, or nation toward a shared vision, then we will need to learn more about consensus. We may need to let go of our own closely held perspective and allow for a common concentric circle which perhaps none of us imagined, but which in the end all share. The Dance of the Dolphin, while concentric, has no predetermined center point; it leaves the centering process with the participants.

At the site or classroom level, consensus on substantive issues is unlikely to be achieved in a single meeting with a boss seeking his predetermined outcome. Rather, it's actively inviting disagreement, thoroughly mixing all the perspectives, and ending with a solid, shared outcome.

Contentedness with the Day

By this point, someone might be saying, I can't do all this! I have a standardized curriculum and accountability for testing to worry about! But there is some very good news: We don't have to do all this. All we have to do is be *willing* to be *open* to what's called for on any given day. That's it. The process will work its own product over time.[4] This is simple and gratifying and even easy, if I'm not preoccupied with regret over something in the past, or with worry over something in the future. Both these preoccupations steal me away from this moment, which makes me unavailable to those around me in the present. This is a very real and common condition. So, we must make peace with our past and future, if we're to do the Dance of the Dolphin in the present.

One simple yet powerful way we can let go of our past hurts and regrets, in order to be fully alive in the present, is to "erase old tapes," that is, let go of bitter memories. "Bitter memories and resentments can be erased by forgiving the people who hurt us," (Mel B. 1996). We might do this by seeing them as more human, and therefore fallible. Maybe we can see that

> you don't need to blame your parents for teaching you to be like them. What else could they teach you but what they know? They did the best they could, and if they abused you, it was due to their own … fears, their own beliefs. They had no control over the programming they received, so they couldn't have behaved any differently. (Ruiz 1997, 104)

Or we might make progress in letting go of the past by trying to identify whether we played any part in the hurtful outcome: Did I make matters worse? Of course, this won't work for many childhood hurts. If it is a childhood memory, it helps me to realize how much younger that adult who hurt me was at the time than I am now, and to remember how little I knew of life at that person's age.

However I let go of past hurts, regrets, and disappointments, let go I must—for myself first, and then for my ability to work with kids. Because as we have made clear, I can't give away what I don't have, and I can't keep what I don't give away. If what I have is freedom from the past, a contentedness with this day, with this moment, then I can give away that contentment to kids who may sorely need a stable adult to be such a touchstone in their lives, an adult to model hope for getting past their own hurts.

The same holds true for living in the future. Much of my own life I couldn't live in the present because I was too busy trying to achieve for the future. We can spot this if we find ourselves thinking, "But I can't be content (rest) today; I haven't achieved

- that changed relationship I want with my spouse/child/parent/sibling/friend
- the lifetime partner I dream of
- my dream job/promotion/salary
- my dream house/car(s)/furnishings
- that dream achievement (that advanced degree, that martial arts ranking, enlightenment)."

Well, what can I do about this today? Trying to live in the past or the future robs us of the peace and joy to be found in this day. And it robs us of what we *can* do toward our goals or dreams. I can't have peace or joy now if I'm worried about the future. I can't have peace or joy now if I'm rehashing things I regret (which is not to say there aren't things I can or should do today to clear up some of my wrecked past, and to lessen that regret).

The Dalai Lama points out two ways to achieve this contentedness, which he terms *happiness*. One way is to have (attain) everything we want. Our society has made heroes of those who have done just that, who have built empires in an effort to have anything and everything they may desire. The trouble is, there will always crop up one more thing they don't have, and so the process is unending. "The second, and more reliable, method is not to have what we want but rather to want and appreciate what we have" (The Dalai Lama and Cutler 1998, 29).

Let's see if we can bring this concept to life. I am going to ask you to indulge me in a small experiment. First, write down three things you would like to achieve. Under each, write out what you can do about them today. Second, write out next to each what you have felt pressured to complete, but which cannot be done today, anyway. Can you see how unrealistic it might have been to try meeting those expectations today? Then ask yourself if it is more helpful to worry about what I can't do, or to find contentment in just doing what I can?

Perhaps a personal example may clarify the concept. At this moment, I have one book and about fifteen articles in print. Of course, I am working on this book, which I wish were finished and in print, something I can't accomplish today. I can only write "one day's worth" of it. Beyond this, I have outlines for at least four more books, and with enough free time, could probably create a handful of good articles a year. Maybe someday that will add up to ten or more books, and 50—or even 100—articles. But those are lifetime goals: I can't live my whole life today. And would I want to? Because if all those goals were met, what would I do tomorrow? So then, I must learn to see and be content with accomplishing today only what is realistic for today, and not be frustrated at not completing my life goals overnight. "Time always seems to pass too slowly or too quickly. We want the fun times to last longer. We want the boring or painful times to go faster. But time goes at just the right pace.... Time is nature's way of keeping everything from happening at once" (Hazelden 1989, June 14). I must want what I have, not strive for what I want, for what I don't have, if I'm going to be present to meet kid's needs, through the Dance of the Dolphin.

Nurturing Courage and Hope

There are those who have been beaten and then trodden under by the educational system (Kennedy 2001d), who have little reason to trust it or any of us who are a part of it. Sometimes we may need to silently communicate our hope for them; sometimes we may need to say words of encouragement to them. But however we do it, it is up to us to help them revive hope—to believe that they can make it in school, that school is a place for them, too. For the high schooler who can't read; for the middle schooler who can't do arithmetic; for the primary age learner who just can't see how language and the written alphabet are related, we'll have to have curriculum and instructional tools that work. But even more, we'll also need to convince these kids that these things will work *for them*. We must nurture the courage in them to try one more time.

One of the great myths which Western culture loves is that courage equates to physical prowess—overcoming physical fear or pain, such as in facing an opponent on the playing field, or even on the street (witness our action movies). But these situations really take very little courage—because they hold the promise of glory, and perhaps even adulation. What takes real courage is to have faith. We are asking a child who has been let down by us—that is, by the system we serve—to have faith in that system again, in us, in our society (from which many of them have been excluded). We're asking the child to have courage.

The good news is that this is not impossible. We adults may not deserve the faith these kids will place in us, but we need it. And they will take their cue from us; if they think we really believe they can do it, many will be willing to try—one more time. I learned the saying years ago that people will rise to the level of expectation we set for them. I saw this principle at work in myself in Navy boot camp thirty years ago. Humor me as I tell the story.

One requirement for all recruits was to go through something called "The Gas Chamber." This was an aboveground concrete bunker about 12 feet by 12 feet, and maybe 8 feet high, with one industrial strength door. This door had a single plexiglas window about eye level, which was probably six inches by twelve inches. Oh, and there were pipes running in from the roof, which ended in shower-like nozzles. The test was that about ten of us at a time were told to stand outside the bunker in front of the door where we were given gas masks, which had to be held at our sides until we were ordered to put them on. Then we were shoved inside and the door sealed behind us, at which point the gas began to hiss in through the pipes. We had been instructed to hold our breaths, but still I found my eyes were stinging and watering, my nose and throat burned, and I began to feel very claustrophobic—I didn't even like some of these guys I was sandwiched against! It seemed after a time that I couldn't hold out for another second, but I did so because we were under orders, and to fail to obey was unthinkable (at the very least, I'd have to do it all over again: talk about high stakes testing!).

I heard someone behind me gasp and then fumble with the mask—I knew he'd put it on prematurely and so failed the exercise. Then a few others followed. The instructors were standing at the window watching us, and they began screaming something at these guys—and the rest of us. I couldn't hear what they were saying, but I *knew* what they were saying. A lifetime later, just as I was reaching to put my own mask on regardless of the consequences, the instructors gave the order to attach the masks. As I did so, I found this was only marginally helpful, because there was no way I could suck enough oxygen from the gas-filled bunker, through the filters, to fill my burning lungs. And still, it wasn't over. They made us stand there awhile longer, breathing through those masks. Eventually they opened the door and we all spilled out. I had passed.

Whatever I feel about the military today—or even felt then—I don't hate that experience, nor the men who supervised it. As ugly as it was, I learned from it that I could do things I wouldn't have thought possible. I had risen to the level of expectation someone else had set for me, and learned something important about myself. Those men nurtured courage in me, courage to have faith in a system that I didn't completely understand or previously completely trust. And they nurtured hope—that the gas mask, and the whole exercise, would work.

Of course, I'm not advocating anything of this nature for kids. But I am saying that learning to read at a higher level or to simplify fractions may have something in common with my gas chamber experience. We will have to nurture courage and hope in our young charges by showing our high expectations for them, if we expect them to place their faith in us one more time. And of course, anything less than their trying one more time is unthinkable.

Exhibiting Patience

One day many years ago my family and I visited a car dealership in search of the American Dream. This was during what I now call my Big Shot days; I was making a six-figure income as an early-thirty-something, and wanted the whole world to know it. Only something really flashy would do. Being in marketing myself, I had no patience for the car salesman who hastily approached. Judging by appearances (which I usually did), both he and his clothes had seen better days. My out-of-control ego, combined with my belief that I knew all his "tricks" already and didn't need his spiel, caused me to be very short with him. When he persisted, I yelled at him to "hit the bricks."

Now that I'm decades older and perhaps marginally wiser, I see that what was really going on was not that I knew he and I were different; rather, I was afraid we weren't—and with a few bad months, I could easily become him, maybe was already closer than I wanted to admit. In fact, I was evidently so fearful of this that I couldn't even let him finish a sentence. If I had been more secure with my own situation, admitting that at the moment I was financially on top of the world, but that could change in a flicker; if I had been less self-absorbed, and more attuned to the fact that I am not the center of the universe, that others, whatever their station in life, are no less important than I; if I had been more comfortable within my own skin, happier with who I was at that moment instead of always needing to achieve more in order to prove my worth—then I might have been able to exhibit patience to this poor fellow who was only trying to earn a living.

Patience in the teacher who has learned to be a leader/follower may mean, for example, that a traditionalist teacher in a traditional site or system allows the unconventional learner, the innovator or communicator, time to ask and resolve for himself that the teacher's new curricular unit leaves room for his progressive or personalistic outlook. Or, it may mean pausing for a moment for an immature student to stop a clowning episode and allow the class to continue. Or, it may mean allowing the high school student who reads at the second grade level to say "pass" when chosen to read out loud. It may mean postponing that lecture or discussion that I really wanted to cover today, in order to capitalize on a teachable moment. Or, patience may mean I put up with a particularly obnoxious student—that I give my best to him, just as I do the pliable, scholarly, or giving student—even when it takes many months, even all year, before I begin to see him mature into a less obnoxious state.

I seem to get at least my share of such year-long projects, and maybe this is only right, given my own lack of patience earlier in my life. At any rate, it's fairly easy for me to create a scenario to illuminate how this concept might play out. Let's call our "project" James—a 15-year-old who's been given up on by most previous teachers. When James comes to my class for the first time, he is not a criminal (yet), although some might quip he is criminally obnoxious. He is very bright, and even a traditional learner. He has a quick, biting wit, and an uncanny ability to judge how far he can go without crossing the line that will get him into Big Trouble. He can take what someone is saying and twist it to make it funny, then stretch that right up to everyone's breaking point. Sometimes, however, he misjudges that point, or some witty saying pops out that is really harassment. Then, James is on his way again.

So when James came to my class, the adults in his life had all been stretched beyond the breaking point. The other students in my class, knowing him from previous settings, groaned when they saw him walk in with the admission slip. But while I certainly don't enjoy difficulties, I have believed for some time that exhibiting patience was part of being a good teacher leader/follower. Thus James and I set to work. And in fact, James turned out to have much to offer me and his classmates (which is not to say it was always fun or easy to work with him). He went on to become successful in class and to return to a regular high school where he earned a diploma.

Drawing Healthy Boundaries

One way I work with kids like James, and a reason I can expect them to change from immature class clowns to mature class participants, and so become people I can not only lead but sometimes even follow, is that I've learned the importance of boundaries. Much of childhood, especially adolescence, is a time of testing limits. In fact, this is a part of a child's identity formation, called individuation, at a developmental stage called "identity formation versus role confusion" (Erikson 1968). This central fact in the adolescent's life makes this a confusing time. She may struggle, for example, with questions such as: What rules (and even laws) are good? Which are good/important for me? If I break the rules my parents/guardians have set, who will I become? Is rule breaking a big/important part of the identity I'm forming? I want to separate from the adults in my life, so how much do I rebel/anger them with my rule breaking? Will they still love me?

I believe that what kids need during this time is for adults to be adults—not to be swept up into their world of chaotic, confusing thoughts and feelings (remember, the adolescent body is producing hormones at warp speed). What kids need is for adults who don't blame or shame them for being sometimes inconsistent, sometimes rebellious, generally confused, acting out of character at times, insecure, emotionally needy, angry about the biological things happening to them that they can't control or understand. What kids desperately need is someone who understands and empathizes with their situation, but refuses to be drawn into it; someone who can tell them where the safe limits are, and explain what could happen to them if they ignore those limits.

I have seen kids who don't understand or just plain ignore these limits and suffer myriad consequences: declining grades; estrangement from adults (parents, a favorite teacher or coach); loss of friends; poor health, addictions (such as to drugs, alcohol, too much food / too little food, rage, violence, and sex, just to mention a few [Kennedy 2001b]); incarceration; and even death. The business of drawing healthy boundaries, or limits, is a serious, even life-saving one. It has to do with holding kids in high regard, and expecting them to emerge from childhood as healthy adults. These high expectations—remembering that making mistakes is a part of learning how to live—will mirror a teacher's high respect, and give authenticity to the boundaries set.

Here is an example of a time when I set and enforced boundaries with kids. A couple of my best students took exception to an assignment I made late on a Friday afternoon. Their solution was to copy from each other, which both knew, having been in my class for quite some time, is something that pushes my buttons. Wrong answers I have no problem with; right answers copied from another student send me into orbit. When I first began to suspect what these two were doing, I gave the whole class a general warning to "do your own work." Evidently determined to make me back down, and perhaps believing that I had so much time invested in them that I wouldn't enforce my own boundary, these two threw me petulant looks and continued to (now blatantly) copy.

While my class often operates in the dance steps of commitment and community, this was a case that definitely called for me to demand compliance. The resulting action I took was fairly traditional and involved some old-fashioned punishment, including transfers to other classes. Of course, the following Monday both offenders were tearfully regretful and pleaded for mercy. But I believe leniency and mercy are sometimes different, and in this case the former would have been counterproductive. These two kids needed me to be the adult and show that the strong boundaries I had set in the area of academic honesty were not negotiable, that my respect for their abilities would hold even when it cost all of us. Of course, both did well in their new classes and eventually went on to more traditional schools. But before leaving, each came to see me, to say "thank you" and give me a hug. This showed me that they knew what it had cost me to draw and enforce boundaries, and at least intuited that it was an important part of their healthy development.

Protecting the Idealism and Enthusiasm of Youth

The ideal. Most of us adults have pretty much given up on it. I guess that's where the saying, the idealism of youth, originates. In fact, idealism is inherent in at least one stage of youth, adolescence. It is part of their natural development (Biehler and Snowman 1990), a time of asking "Why not?" It is about different life possibilities—and specifically about the possibilities for their own lives. Not every kid can be President of the United States or play in the NBA, but if we encourage them to follow their dreams, most will realize they don't want to be President or play professional sports. When they learn to recognize their own voice, they'll know that those things are others' passions, not theirs.

What I am saying is that adults must allow them to dream big, to try out different directions without adults telling them no, or that they can't do it. Life will limit their choices enough without our help. Instead, we need to encourage them as they soar through the myriad possibilities that seem open to them, to find that one overriding passion and pursue it. I can count on the fingers of one hand the number of people who responded with a straight face when I told them I was writing my first book. I could read their minds: "But you're just a teacher! You're not a college professor; you don't have a doctorate; you haven't the right pedigree to do such a thing. At your age, haven't you outgrown the idealism of youth?" Evidently not, because that first book became a reality—as has the second.

Idealism is what allows kids to dream big dreams; it gives them the courage to pursue their passions. If no adult in their lives has the courage to hope the best for kids—even if it means they'll go farther than that adult has gone or ever will go—they may lose their best opportunity for identifying their real interests. At least one adult needs to have the patience to allow them to be children for the few short years they have without squelching their hope with a grumbling, "They need to be realistic," or "I just don't want them to get hurt." Without the chance idealism offers, kids may not explore for their passion, the generative spark they can uniquely offer the ever-unfolding universe.

Listening to and Learning from Students

"To listen to someone who has no one to listen to him is a very beautiful thing," Mother Teresa taught us (Gonzalez-Balado 1996, 94). This is perhaps the most important thing we need to do as classroom leaders. Listening to someone without preoccupation, without distraction, focused only on that person—is an extremely fulfilling experience for the speaker. This experience has the effect of validating the person listened to, of underscoring their existence, of telling them that they matter in this world, have a place in it, are not some accident, unwanted, unloved. To listen to someone, especially a young person who has no one else at that moment, is a beautiful thing (Nation and Stevenson 2001).

Try to recall a time when you really needed to talk, and you found someone willing to listen: a spouse, child, friend, colleague, boss, stranger. Someone who put everything aside, physically and mentally, so that they were present and focused on listening to you; not finishing your sentences for you, not interrupting you, just listening. *Can* you recall such a time? There are not many people in our lives who can or will do this for us. It requires the listener to sacrifice all egocentric concerns, all the other things he or she might want to be doing.

Listening, not partially but fully, is a truly selfless act. And there aren't many people in any of our lives who can be truly selfless on our behalf. But then, it doesn't require many. And it doesn't require many for the kids we serve, either—perhaps only one. We might become that one person for some of them. If I can stop my busy-ness and my preoccupation for a moment to listen to the kid right in front of me, the experience can be intensely rewarding for both of us.

I learned this, like most of what little I know, from experience. It began the day Charlie came to class totally distraught over the fight he'd just had with his father. I attempted to smooth it over so we could get on with the class, but Charlie was not to be mollified. At the time, I was fortunate to have an alternative education classroom with some flexibility in the schedule. This allowed me to set a course for the rest of the class, and to take Charlie to a corner where he and I could sit and talk. Or rather, where Charlie could talk—which he did for two hours—while I listened. When I would try to murmur something encouraging, he waved it off and kept talking; he didn't need me to talk; he needed me to listen. He didn't want my advice, my perspective, my "wisdom"; he only wanted to be validated: to know it was OK for him to be who he was, to *be* at all, to occupy a place on this earth despite what he believed others were telling him or how he might feel about that. At such times, I like to remember Rabbi Heschel's (2001, 62-63) admonition that we need *textpeople* in place of *textbooks;* that kids need to be able to read *us* as plumb lines for living.

To achieve moments like this with Charlie and others like him, I must be willing to take the heat for giving students time to get their personal needs met, and not be exclusively focused on the tasks of learning; to allow them to be validated through their experience instead of rigidly insisting on efficiently covering standardized tasks like learning lists of facts. In reality, I believe that taking the time for people while setting aside tasks will actually lead to more efficiency, not less.

But this will take faith in the belief that it is possible to synthesize the two sides of the Great Debate. Doing the full Dance of the Dolphin in this way will involve risk taking by the teacher—or administrator. The more that students who have previously lacked success in school can experience success under a courageous teacher and/or administration (Mercogliano 1998), the more those adults are open to attacks from the militantly traditionalist camp.

First, break all the rules (Buckingham and Coffman 1998) may be the best advice anyone could give a teacher who seeks to transition from a one-sided, one- or two-step dance, which always produce the mediocre results we are having with altogether too many students, to the amazing results we first dreamed of when we chose this profession. And the first rule to be broken is to again have time to listen to and learn from kids.

Living According to Our Beliefs

This may be the most central idea in this chapter: We as individuals need to be integrated. We must be genuine and authentic, not for others, but for ourselves. We won't have the strength to carry on otherwise. We must integrate beliefs and actions.

I went through several "professions" before finally coming to education. That's because I was afraid to act on, or even acknowledge, that I was created to be a teacher. Other people "told" me it was crazy to settle for a third of the money I could be making (this usually just played in my head as a "tape," not spoken overtly, but scrabbled together from a lifetime of body language, innuendo, and stony silence) to live with a low-status career. Of course, the low status we in the West have for the profession is a very public "secret," despite what we say we believe. We show our attitude toward children by the amount of time we choose to give to them; and in turn, we show the value we have for children in the esteem (and yes, salary is one indicator) we give those who work with them.

Even as I sit here in a favorite coffee shop writing this, a gentleman at another table, obviously on a leisurely outing with his wife and grown daughter, turns to me and asks, "Are you a teacher?" (Am I wearing a sign, or does he simply recognize something in the demeanor?) A part of me cringes to be publicly identified; today, *teacher* is even more pejorative than it used to be, teachers having become the favorite whipping boy of the politicians and media for our "failing schools" (Kennedy 2001c). But giving a fearful response would be living out the beliefs of someone else for me, not *my* deeply held convictions. I run through this whole stream of consciousness in the blink of an eye and then answer, "Yes, I am." This response is loaded with what is not said: No, I have not moved "up" from being "just a teacher" to become something less distasteful to the public: a principal, superintendent, college professor. While I have done some of those things, they are not my passion; they do not fulfill my most deeply held beliefs about what I most want to accomplish in the flicker that is my lifetime on this earth.

> We must remind ourselves that though our lives are small and our acts seem insignificant, we are generative elements of this universe, and we create meaning with each act that we perform or fail to perform.... It is here, on this earth, in the day to day, on the street corner, at our evening table, in the homes of our friends, at the bedside of the sick, in the arms of

> our wife or husband, in the warmth or sadness of our child's days, that the universe is being formed.
>
> Far from being a great system and puzzle that we are asked to comprehend, [this universe] is a dynamic, ever-changing reality that we can influence by our every act and gesture (Nerburn 1999, 87).

Teaching every day is the life which gives me the most opportunity to add my generative element to the ever-forming universe. I cannot afford to allow the perceptions of others, even well-meaning friends or the collective weight of an entire public, to steal the meaningfulness from my life.

But given the daily assault on the "the state of education" or "the way education has failed us," how can I know for sure that being a teacher is right for me? Perhaps by answering a few simple questions: Am I teaching because it's my passion—or because it's someone else's vision of where I "fit?" Am I aware of my deepest held beliefs about life in general and about my own life? How are these connected to my profession and its practical applications (the site/assignment in which I practice)? Am I able to practice my deepest held beliefs about what education is and should be at this site/in this classroom? If I could live my life over, who would I become? If the answer is not who/what I am today, what needs to change? If I were 95 years old, sitting on the porch rocking and reviewing my life, what would I regret? The answers to these questions will provide the keys to whether or not I'm acting out my deepest held beliefs and making my unique contribution to this dynamic, open-ended universe.

There are several things that can keep me from acting on my beliefs, of not living an integrated life. Perhaps first is fear. Fear of what people will say if I go against the majority or take an unpopular stance by choosing a low-status profession. A second obstruction may be attachments. If I've gotten into the habit of not dealing with my deeper feelings by escaping to something else when they threaten to pop up—for example, by abusing alcohol, legal or illegal drugs, spending or hoarding money, overeating, misuse of sexuality, trying to control others, or in fact *anything* to ignore deep (we might say chronic) feelings—these can produce shame in me (May 1988). This truth stems from the fact that I turn to one of these numbing agents to keep from feeling the hurt of not being at peace with acting according to my own deeply held beliefs.

A third element that can hinder me from following my dreams is regret at parts of my past or denial of important parts of myself which I feel must be denied (killed off) along with the dream which nurtured them. While we touched on making peace with our past in an earlier section, it applies again here. For example, at one time I dreamt of returning to the military as a chaplain. When this dream didn't materialize, I cut myself off from much of what was meaningful to me. One result was that I ended up in business—not because I liked it, but probably more out of confusion—and consequently gave up many of the things I had earlier studied and enjoyed (such as the history of ideas and study of languages), thinking that there was no place in my life for those things anymore. Now that I'm older, I see that the things I enjoy don't have to fit neatly into my profession/calling; they can just be for their own sake. And I need to acknowledge what they are and nurture them as a part of me if I hope to be genuine to myself and live according to my beliefs. To complete the illustration using my personal journey, after leaving business to enter teaching, all those things once again came into play—and all the books I'd given away because I "had no more use for them"—were sorely missed. Perhaps if I had read these words of Ruiz (1997, 106-108), I could have avoided many mistakes:

> The first step toward personal freedom is awareness. We need to be aware that we are not free in order to be free … there is no reason to suffer. With awareness you can rebel and say, "This is enough!" You can look for a way to heal and transform your personal dream. It is not even real. If you go into the dream and start challenging your beliefs, you will find that most of the beliefs that guided you into the wounded mind are not even true. You will find that you suffered all those years of drama for nothing. Why? Because the belief system that was put inside your mind is based on lies.
>
> That is why it is important for you to master your own dream; that is why the Toltecs became dream masters. Your life is the manifestation of your dream; it is an art. And you can change your life anytime if you aren't enjoying the dream. Dream

masters create a masterpiece of life; they control the dream by making choices. Everything has consequences and a dream master is aware of the consequences.

Conclusion

As we have seen, the traditional view of the teacher's supervision role has been the one-sided classroom management model, the teacher-as-boss. But at the same time, a one-sided reaction to this traditionalist view in which the teacher is nothing more than another student, is equally deficient. In the Dance of the Dolphin, however, the teacher is at times a leader, at times a follower. This means going beyond an either/or dichotomous view,[5] and integrating the two, which allows them to flow as one dance. As we demonstrated beginning in Chapter One, both Traditional and Unconventional views of running the classroom are important. The challenge for the educator is to do *both*, gracing the classroom and those who populate it with a living exemplar of the best of both worlds, and modeling an ability to operate in either of them. In the process, we will be meeting the leadership challenge.

Becoming both a leader and a follower in the classroom may seem to be a challenging, even impossible concept at first. But we have seen the answer to this obstacle in the characteristics necessary for doing the Dance of the Dolphin: Each day is its own journey, and who of us can achieve perfection, all our life goals, dreams, aspirations in this one day? None of us, of course. So that's the answer: We are not to be a perfect *product* before we can become leaders/followers; we need only be in the messy *process* of life, living the adventure that is today, not reliving all the yesterdays nor fretting over all the tomorrows. Although very simple, this concept is so foreign to the modern mind that it may take some getting used to.

I have been helped in the attempt by the authors cited along the way in the text, and by reading some of the wisdom literature from various spiritual traditions. I first realized that being a co-learner, at times a follower of those whom at other times I lead, requires some measure of humility on my part. While I would never suggest that I have learned any humility, it has helped to read such things as "We grow small trying to be great" (E. Stanley Jones in Hazelden Foundation 1989, July 19 entry). When Mother Teresa was asked how she felt about the people who said they could see God in her, she answered that that made her happy, but that her purpose was to see God in others, and "especially in those who suffer" (Gonzalez-Balado 1996, 87), in which category she would include children: "Children are so very, very lonely!" (Mother Teresa 1989, 124).

A further concept to consider is that many of the ten characteristics we have highlighted as essential for the teacher as leader/follower are things that will probably be more caught than taught. This implies that those of us who desire to accept the challenge must be willing to let go of trying to control the outcome of the educational enterprise, as well as the outcome of many things in our own lives, and leave room for mystery. We must be willing to be changed ourselves before trying to change the world. Socrates admonished, "Let him who would move the world, first move himself" (Hazelden Information and Education Service 1989, August 4). But let's not think it is some self-help program I'm advocating; rather it is an openness to the invitation of the universe to rejoice in co-creating what the new day is to become, not enslaved by some self-improvement goal but work that is so much "us" that it becomes play, the living of our dreams. "We need to approach life in a relaxed manner, letting the natural rhythm of events take over and do some of the work for us. Too much effort defeats itself" (Mel B. 1996, January 28).

If there is power in acknowledging and being patient with the process of life; if there is power in having the humility to let go of the control which we don't have anyway; if there is greatness not in how others see us, but in how we see others; then, becoming a leader/follower must be a part of the answer in how we become the teachers we want to be. Will we have the insight and clarity of mind to reshape old perspectives? Will we have the courage to admit our humanity before our followers? Will we have the humility to view our students in ways that allow us to see their greatness? Merely beginning the journey to do these things is demonstration that we have taken up the leadership challenge. The next chapter will begin to give us some practical ways for beginning the Dance of the Dolphin in our classrooms.

Notes

1. I call this Step One only because it is probably the oldest of the views, not because it has any primacy in status.

2. In fact, many of our social structures are based on this most basic of human organizations: the family and/or the extended family. An easy reference is to think of the history we've read wherein a king or chieftain is addressed as Great Father or Sire. And we could investigate the etymologies of other words, such as patriarch, matriarch, patron. While I understand and apologize for these examples being sexist, they come from history, which *is* sexist. But that aside, the point is: What could be more basic than the origin of life itself, which springs from parents, and their parents, and by extension, aunts, uncles, cousins, etc.

3. I was first introduced to this concept at the University of La Verne Teacher Leader Conference in 1994 by Tom Harvey.

4. In truth, every day will be a slightly different, ever-improving "product," some might say "snapshot" of the process.

5. Part of the reason for this is that the choice is not as broad as it may appear on the surface. The "new" style of management, called Leadership, often seems to me to be only the old view in disguise: how to be a better boss. In other words, it's still top-down, with the boss manipulating people, events, timeframes to be more efficient—in the task, in the doing. No mention is made of the human/humane or the spiritual side of life or of leadership. That is, leadership is code for gathering more influence to oneself in order to achieve a product more quickly, effortlessly, or brilliantly.

Reality Checks

1. The Lakota have a saying; "The ones that matter most are the children. They are the true human beings" (Zona 1994, 49). Can you list some ways you have let society's expectations and messages carry you away from the "true" you? Can you name at least one thing which you dreamed of as a child, which is no longer part of your life?

2. "It is only humans who fetter themselves with the chains of past and future; animals experience a continual present," teaches Caitlin Matthews from the Celtic tradition (1999, 371). Can you list three things which you wish were different about your past? If they were partly your fault, can you discuss with a friend some realistic options for how you might make them right? If they were not your fault, can you see any good that came out of them, even if it seems coincidental? How important are

those good things to you? How much did they alter the course of your life for the positive?

3. "Our actions tell us if we're leading a spiritual life. What do you do when you see someone in need? Spirituality means helping. It's not just kind words" (Hazelden 1989, October 12). What are three ways you might show spirituality in your classroom today? This year?

4. Can you think of something you'd like to change about your outlook, but don't know if you can do it permanently? Maybe have more patience with a difficult student; maybe not respond when an obnoxious colleague or administrator baits you; maybe refute those old messages that were put in your head in childhood, and which erode your confidence or sense of worth. An old saying is, "Just for today." What if you try to change that one thing just for today?

Chapter Three

The Leadership Challenge

Delegating to Student Leadership

In the Dance of the Dolphin, as we've seen, there will be times when the teacher is in the traditionally superordinate position, and the student the subordinate spot. But there will be other times when the teacher will occupy the learner—or subordinate—position. Sometimes this might be because one student or group is leading a class activity, with teacher as observer. Often at such times, however, the teacher is still directing the class: leading the dance, so to speak. There will be other times, though, when the teacher will be dancing, or engaged, with a smaller group than the whole class, perhaps even with one individual student. During these times, how can I as the teacher be assured that the rest of the class keeps functioning? Who is leading the dance for those with whom I am not engaged at that time? Who is keeping an eye on things—because after all, we can't be so utopian as to believe that *every* child will be fully engaged at all times without any imminent adult presence. We are going to need help to ensure that things run smoothly without the teacher as centerpiece.

The answer to this dilemma is found in our original metaphor: It takes both leader and follower, dolphin and human, to complete the circle. As we said in Chapter One, as dolphin and man made this circle they alternated the ascendent and descendent position, moving seamlessly from one to the other. Just to restate one principle of the Dance of the Dolphin, then, it is not our job as teacher to always be a top-down manager, always the centerpiece, always the sage on the stage. It is not a case of either being in control or not being in control, of either ironclad control or anarchy. The former focuses exclusively on the privilege of power, the latter on relinquishing all power—and responsibility. We can afford neither singular focus.

> In our time, many people are resentful of *privilege* whenever they encounter it, seeing only one half of the contract that privilege entails.... The *responsibility* of caring for and not abusing (those) under our charge is a heavy one.
>
> Keeping to our own part, to our own duties, enables us to be part of the whole. *It is not one person's task to do everything.* With our emphasis on the nuclear family, we have lost the close sense of community whereby everyone contributes something and has his or her place. Instead, we aim to be superpeople. (Matthews 1999, 17 March; *emphasis mine*)

It is not one person's duty to do everything. This is the crux of inviting students into the Dance of the Dolphin. The teacher is not tasked to do everything, to be a superperson. Instead, the teacher is asked to forego that mindset and let everyone in the classroom contribute something, to have a place of ownership. Some will have places of lesser responsibility, so that they can more freely focus on their own needs. A few will have places of more responsibility, encompassing responsibility for others, and with that will come the additional freedom necessary to carry out these responsibilities. This chapter is about finding the latter: those students who are ready, able, and willing to learn to become protégés in sharing overall supervisory responsibilities with the teacher—to become Micro Leaders.

I have taken the order in which we will approach this discussion from the perspective of the old adage that prescribes what seems to me to represent the most healthy order for living: *be, do, have*. That is, if I first focus on *what I want to be*, my personal meaning and desired qualities, then I will find it natural to *act on or do them*, providing the authority for expecting my students to follow suit; and finally, I will probably discover that I "suddenly" *have what I want*. In the classroom it plays out in this way: who I *am* will strongly influence what I and student leaders *do*, which in turn will affect what we *have* together, which will in all likelihood turn out to be that which we all wanted to have anyway. So in this sense, this chapter begins where the previous one left off, with who we educators are.

Be: My Prerequisite Attitude

In Chapter Two we discussed who I will want and need to be, or rather want to be in the process of becoming, in order to have the freedom to allow myself to enter the Dance of the Dolphin and gain the ability to relinquish the almost total privilege that I have as the teacher and to share that privilege with students. It is important to add to the discussion, however, the principle that I believe drives the need for delegating privilege and responsibility: Anything one of my protégés can do almost as well as I can, I need to delegate to them. This is healthy for me, and it's essential for them.

It's healthy for me to delegate because I'm admitting I can't do everything and it frees me from having to try. "We need to approach life in a relaxed manner, letting the natural rhythm of events take over and do some of the natural work for us. Too much effort defeats itself" (Mel B. 1996, Jan 28). We don't need to try so hard to be something that someone else has told us we should be or do. Life is not a self-help program, where we need to achieve others' ideals and goals for us. It's much easier than that. Rather, life is merely staying open to the moment and living out what comes our way. "When you chop wood, chop wood," an ancient Taoist proverb reminds us.

For example, when I am listening to one needy student, I can relax and focus on that person. It is obviously not helpful to that student if I am distracted by the myriad things going on in the room that could concern me at that moment—because then I'm present to none of them. At that moment, I don't need to worry that there are other needy students in my class, that there are papers to grade, administrative forms to fill out, standards to deal with, that my next book or article requires more work, that I may owe money on my taxes or car insurance. I believe this is what Prystowsky (2002, 3) is saying when he exhorts us to live by "honoring others in the moment, or, loving without regard to outcome" Hope plays a big part in developing this perspective:

> Hope is believing good will come, even in bad times.... Hope is knowing that no matter how afraid we are, God will be with us. Hope is knowing that we never have to be alone again. It is knowing that time is on our side. Hope is giving up control. Hope is knowing we never had control in the first place. (Hazelden 1989, March 23)

If I can embrace this outlook, then I don't have to strive. Because striving implies ignoring the fullness of what's in front of me at the moment and trying to live in and control the future, feats that no one has ever been able to accomplish.

Here is a personal example which may help. In my mid-40s, still tuned in to many "should" voices, I enrolled in and earned a master's degree in educational administration. This would have been fine had it been one of my dreams. But the truth is, my passion has always been teaching. While I could perhaps achieve some level of success in administration, it's not something I have wanted to do. At 50, finally realizing this, I began to allow myself to hope that following my passion was enough. I realized that attempting to rigidly control my fate—my "success"—especially in an effort to please others, had been killing my hope.

Being honest with myself that I'm a teacher—"just" a teacher to many hard chargers in our society—allowed me to let go of trying to do, to achieve, in order to satisfy others' dreams. What followed was amazing: A whole series of wonderful things began—all within six months of making peace with the reality that my passion was teaching.

- A teachers association selected me to become a high risk youth trainer of trainers for the entire state (this is a highly selective process, and I had not really thought I'd have a chance to be chosen).

- A university for which I formerly taught part-time made sweeping changes and, out of the blue, the new progressive administration called to ask me to return.

- Leaders in the martial art that I study asked me to consider becoming an instructor.

- This book was accepted for publication, which showed me and others that my first book was not a fluke.
- Five new articles were published.
- The mutual respect, admiration, and trust that existed between my students and myself seemed to reach an altogether new plateau.

I recount these things certainly not out of ego, but to make the point how profoundly I've been influenced by the idea, "When you chop wood, just chop wood," and its corollary that living in the moment fosters hope, while worrying about and striving to control the future kills that hope. Releasing the burden of striving to achieve things that I didn't really want anyway resulted in other people, with whom I was more like-minded all along, asking me to be part of things I really *did* want. My being comfortable in my own skin in the present moment, my being true to who I really *am,* led to opportunities to *do* the things I was really passionate about, which led to me *having* the things the real me wanted.

At first, letting go of the "should" voices, of the expectations of others in order to be true to ourselves, and to be present in the moment without feeling driven to do more with it than is possible, can be painful. We might feel a sense of loss, a feeling of our lives being cut back, perhaps invoking the imagery of pruning. But "pruning concentrates the savor of the fruit we bear, for it proceeds from inward peace and promotes outward goodness" (Mogabgab 2001, 3).

No longer striving for control of the outcome of things generates hope and sets the stage for the ability to delegate the other way I can balance privilege and responsibility as a classroom leader. If my hope is in letting go, then in a real sense, my hope for all my own dreams and aspirations to come true for others is in delegating. Further, my delegating to students demonstrates to them that they are worthy to be entrusted with important decisions, that I trust them to grow into delegators themselves, thereby engendering hope for them and then, in turn, for those they will lead. We see how our *being* true to ourselves results in our *doing* for others. This doing begins with choosing and investing in our student leaders, in making them our protégés.

Do: Investing in Protégés. Hope through Emotional Equity

The first thing I must acknowledge is that a commitment to delegating, to viewing select students as protégés, will require an emotional investment in these budding Micro leaders. Like all investments, this one will involve risk taking because it will require us to trust these junior partners with material decisions. What significant things might I be risking with such trust? Matters as important as my reputation, the class dynamic, and even control of the class.

> Like it or not, life seems to have certain risks that just can't be avoided. [Many people] are not really comfortable with risk taking ... especially in situations that include risk of rejection, risk of defeat, or risk of loss.
>
> We might surprise ourselves by succeeding more times than we fail. But even in temporary failure, we gain if we followed through in accepting reasonable and necessary risks. (Mel B. 1996, April 2)

This calculated trust/risk in sharing power with students will pay large dividends and increase the equity we share in the success of the class. "The more the classroom culture respects students, the more students will respect the purpose, principles, and people in the classroom" (Kennedy 1996b, 16).

In other words, when the things entrusted *are* really important, there is true risk not just to them but to me, which makes the act of trust real. Class leaders know that I am viewing them as partners: I as senior partner, they as junior partners. This means that I'm vested in their success; I care about them succeeding, which gives our relationship an almost familial sense. "When you invest real power and real responsibility in your best people and support them with your best methods, everyone has emotional equity in getting results" (Watson and Brown 2001, 31-32).That is, not only am I vested in their success, but they are vested in mine. We both have equity positions in our joint enterprise. "Remembering that respect in a democracy encompasses both freedom and responsibility, the more respect we lavish on students, the more they reciprocate by living up to our expectations" (Kennedy 1996b, 19). This is truly the beginning of the Dance of the Dolphin. Student hope generated through emotional equity in the teacher's/class's success, is prerequisite to the efficacy of student leaders, not just in their Micro jobs, but in their lives as well. This is not the end of the story, however. There are three common obstacles to this success, as we will see next.

Developing Efficacy in Micro Leaders

Dealing with the Past

In my experience, by early adolescence the pasts of most children are strewn with many major disappointments, regrets, and painful memories. This is true for kids from fairly healthy families as well as for those we might classify as high risk. The specifics may change, but the principle does not. These regrets will usually wear on the child, making him or her feel it was their own failing that led to this happening to them. The result is a downward spiral in self-image and their sense of self-worth. If left unchallenged, these feelings and beliefs about themselves will only deepen, so that they eventually become part of the child's permanent beliefs about his or her past; and they will often persist into young adulthood. In short, they may believe that "My past is ruined, and there's nothing I can do about it." This hopelessness easily turns to resentment, and resentment is deadly to emotional, spiritual, and physical health. "Resentment is the 'number one' offender. It destroys more (people) than anything else" (Anonymous 1976; 6).

Compounding this regret over their past, children will often seek unhealthy ways to numb the pain of not being able to live with memories of the past, or being able to change it. In order to protect oneself from this pain, to anesthesize it, the human spirit looks for ways to cope. Very often for adolescents, these ways are unhealthy. For example, for pre-, early-, and full adolescents, some of these "solutions" are sexual intimacy, substance abuse, rage, underachievement, overachievement, materialism (hoarding, going into debt, gambling, stealing), and the possibility of becoming part of a gang or tagging/party crew (Kennedy, 2001b). It is somewhat interesting to note the paradox that as a society, we attack these "solutions" and often even the children who choose them, when in fact the youngsters are merely trying to cope with the pain of a past that society itself may have had much to do with causing.

But the cause and misguided solutions of kids' regret at the past is not our main focus here. Instead, we bring it up only to point out that this is the reality for many kids and that, as teachers, we need to find a way to help them put as much of their regret to rest as possible. Until we can lay the past to rest, we cannot live in the present. I don't have a silver bullet to offer for how to help kids deal with the past. Perhaps the closest I've come is suggesting four steps for reversing the negative cycle or spiral that begins with regret, turns to chronic emotional and spiritual pain, and results in the "solutions" we mentioned above. These four steps are: Examining my own life, perhaps by asking if I am the person/worker/friend I would want; what pains the child/adolescent most about their person or life; what are they using to numb the pain; and what can I do to help revise the painful plot line. (Kennedy 2001b)

It is probably unrealistic to expect this to fully resolve a kids' desire for his or her past to be different. In fact, I believe that *most* of us long for different pasts, unless or until we find a way to release the regrets and forgive the offenders (especially those who were adults when we were still children). But if life is a journey instead of a destination, we can at least begin to help alter the paths the kids are currently taking.

Living in the Present

Once our potential Micro leaders, perhaps with our help, are able to escape the constant pain of regret over the past, they can begin to be present. I don't mean physically present—that is easy, and can be a form of compliance. I mean they can be present emotionally and spiritually. This is absolutely essential, both for their own health, and for their ability to lead others in the Micro system.

Part of living in the present will be living with people, in this case other students, who are not as far along in laying their pasts to rest, who will have some bad days, perhaps episodes of "acting out," anti-social behavior, rebellion, or whatever other descriptor we might choose to use. This will be especially true of students who are newer to the class and our Micro system, who are newer to our environment of hope instead of the one of control to which they may have been accustomed in other schools or classes. It will be important for Micro leaders not to be dragged into the cycles of despair of *their* own protégés, the other students.

Nevertheless, there will still be daily adversity as there always is in life. And this will be another area of living in the present in which we may have to coach them. Just as physical injuries will be a part of playing a sport over the long haul, so social-emotional, psychological, and spiritual challenges will be part of nourishing Micro leadership.

Trusting in the Future

As students learn to believe it is OK for them to have their *own* dreams (not "should" messages, not someone else's passion), our encouraging them to give themselves permission to listen to that inner voice that is telling them what their true feelings and passions are, and then to believe they can follow and even achieve that dream—are necessary for our protégés to trust what the future holds and to believe there is hope for them. It is only when they are freed from the longing for a different past, when they can live comfortably in the present, that kids can let go of trying to control the future, and trust—have hope—that it will be OK.

There is one other potential problem with the future which I have seen Micro leaders develop: fear of success. The more failure or problems with school, authorities, or parents that kids have had, the more they will fear success. This is caused by a belief that with their history they can't possibly deserve to succeed, that their success must be a mistake, and is likely to go up in smoke at any moment. They often believe that if anyone really knew their secrets, the world would detest them. Convincing children and adolescents who have broken pasts that they deserve success, is one of the biggest challenges of Micro for you. If we don't watch and prepare for this, we may see our best students self-destruct, as they sabotage themselves right on the cusp of succeeding in a big way. The result can prove devastating for students and us.

Have: Transformation

Reformation versus Transformation

There is a real difference between the call for educational reform and the expectations that we have for it. Therefore, I would like to contrast the concept of reformation with that of transformation. Quite simply, the former seems to me a call for or attempt to return to a former time which "had it right:" to re-form in alignment with the former ideal. Transformation, however, is a call or willingness to be present with—to sit with—a problem until the situation, or we in it, or both, become changed across time (trans-formed). That is, we become different not by trying to eliminate a situation with which we are not happy, or which is painful, but rather through the opposite response of *not* trying to eliminate it, but living with it.

Reformation seems to me tied to the theme of control which we have been weaving through this chapter: an attempt to engineer an anticipated outcome. The problem with this is twofold. First, when dealing with people, things can often seem to be firmly in hand, then quickly slip out of our grasp. We are seeing this, for example, in the attempt to implement academic standards in widespread venues. Second, as we stated earlier, control precludes hope. To put it another way, control rules out mystery, the very idea of possibility. If Einstein had been after the quick answer in order to eliminate mystery, instead of sitting with the mystery, the possibilities that had previously been unthinkable would not have been discovered.

The Beginning of Transformation: Choosing Micro Leaders

To begin this process of transformation, we must choose who will become our student leaders. We obviously must be careful who we choose to entrust with the power and responsibility of Micro leadership; we'll be entering a process and relationship that will forever change them, us, the dynamic between us, and the entire class.

To give you a sense of what I begin to look for in choosing these leader candidates, I would like to refer to Figure 3-1. While you can see that I could have easily turned this into a circular figure to match the dance steps, I tried to keep it simple by following a tabular format. Many readers will want to customize the list; I highly encourage you to do so.

Growth of Micro Leaders

Micro leaders are selected very carefully and entrusted with real, wide-ranging freedoms and responsibilities. Teachers and classmates will be relying on them to facilitate learning, to handle routine logistical class needs, and to help solve peer problems. Leaders will need to appreciate the fact that I, school administrators, district/county-level educators, and even probation officers and juvenile court judges familiar with the program will be expecting them to accept and to demonstrate a significant level of responsibility. For example, when guests visit (such as regional accreditation teams, state auditors, or regional and local educators looking for ideas or simply wanting to check us out), student leaders do the lion's share of the talking. I view this as both a responsibility and a reward for their commitment, sacrifice, and willingness to grow.

Transformation of Micro Leaders: A Rite of Passage

The somewhat unique experience of becoming a Micro leader, because of the depth of challenges which each one will face during their tenure, the resulting growth, and the new confidence and maturity of the leader at the end of the experience, begins a rite of passage for Micro leaders to young adulthood.

The recognition of the universal need for rites of passage often finds expression in a long list of items that are promoted as add-ons to education, both curricular and extra-curricular. Examples of such popular add-ons are service learning, peer mediation, restitution, character education, violence prevention, personal development, anger management, and drug prevention. Micro leaders grow as persons and develop leadership skills more authentically than if they participated in any of these single-focus programs. In a sense, this difference reminds me of the distinction between the theories of *language learning* and *language acquisition*. The former is intentionally, directly taught, while the latter is indirectly acquired, or caught (Cummins 1985; Hakuta 2001; Krashen 1985).

So at a deeper level we might understand these add-on educational programs that many educators are so eager to impose on students as just different facets of the one thing we are really trying to accomplish with kids: their successful passage from one stage of life to the next; from childhood to early adolescence; from adolescence to young adulthood. In earlier generations, these passages were taken out of the adolescent's hands, often through wars. The World War II generation was defined by that catastrophic event; then there was Korea; and of course, Vietnam. So during the decades of the 40s, 50s, and 60s there was no time for extended adolescence. Whether one was for or against the defining event, or not directly involved at all, the events themselves were so large an influence on the whole of society, and so inescapable to the individual that

Figure 3-1
Micro Leader Qualifications

Compliance: *Form*, appearance

- On time (or even early)
- Perfect dress code compliance
- Keep class (or their team) on track according to the learning format
- Not actively engaged in gangs
- Discuss appropriate subjects during class

Conformity: *Function*, skill

- Perfect attendance (come early/stay late)
- Direct facilities cleanup
- Drug and alcohol free—or getting help
- Fulfill Micro obligations effectively
- Competent at orienting new people to the ways of the class
- Lead their subordinates in staying on task

Commitment: *Forward* thinking

- Earn maximum stamps/grades
- Take initiative regularly
- Good sense of social justice

Community: Ensures *fullness* of experience/inclusiveness for all. We are all part of the same world.

- Get along with everyone
- Facilitate social understanding
- Understand that we are all one. What hurts one of us hurts all of us. What helps one of us helps all of us.
- Realize the difference between love and like. Loves all of his/her fellow students, but does not necessarily like them or hang around with them.
- Understand the place that learning perspectives play in collaborative work.

they forced the passage from adolescence to adulthood for many if not most of these generations (Eckert 1998, 251-264, especially 260-261).

But as our very concept of war changed following Vietnam—some would say, because of the disgust and shame by America and its allies at what we had done to others, to ourselves, and to our young—there was perhaps another change: War no longer provided the instant rite of passage from adolescence to adulthood. Now adolescence had time to linger; passage to adulthood could take more time, and perhaps as a result, it became less definite. The downside is that many of our young people have gotten stuck in a prolonged adolescence: living at home longer or "bouncing back"; unable to make adult commitments, such as to a career, a life mate, or even a college major; choosing for whom to vote, or even whether to vote. This situation has prompted many to search for new/old rites of passage, ways to formalize the passage to adulthood, and to ask

> How can we help our young, who wait to cross the frontier, between child and adulthood?... In Celtic society children were frequently given in fosterage to neighboring families so that this transition (rite of passage) could be overseen by adults who were not blood kindred, who had a good sense of some special skill into which the child could be inducted. The custom of fosterage also put a buffer zone between child and parent, thus avoiding the worst of the acrimonious generational confrontations that plague families during adolescence. (Matthews 1999; 23 February)

Educators willing to mentor adolescent protégés are perhaps in a special position to guide their charges through the passage from childhood to young adulthood. Many heavily promoted standalone programs promote an agenda that we desire for young people. But instead of fragmenting life by teaching them as different parts of life, most of these things are acquired naturally, all of a piece in the whole of life, by Micro leaders. Micro leadership acts naturally as a rite of passage.

Student Micro leadership will take the student to his/her next developmental level in life. I have found that Micro leaders will exit the experience as different people, at a different level in their lives. One of the elements necessary to a successful rite of passage seems to be for the person to see the seriousness of their situation, in some cases, the danger (as in the "war" decades we mentioned), or at least to comprehend the reality of mortality (Mahdi, Christopher and Meade 1996). One must have considered life and death matters, and what may be worthy of mortal commitment. "There are three things for which a person might hazard his/her life and lose it: the search for truth, the upholding of justice, the performance of mercy" (Matthews 1999; 24 March). The seriousness of the Micro leadership rite of passage will make the student leader more interested in and capable of truth, justice, and mercy. This is quite a change from the self-absorption of adolescence—and of life lived by Western standards. (We might just think of television advertising as a benchmark of what those standards are: how much truth, justice, and mercy do TV commercials generally promote?)

So, if I am focused on becoming who it is I truly want to become; if my student leaders are then allowed, encouraged, and expected to do what is just in order to ensure that all in the class have the opportunity to succeed in the Dance of the Dolphin; then what we will have is an environment that is merciful for all. This statement also describes the how-to for guiding these student leaders through this passage.

Standalone programs would seem to tell us we need a list of steps, a manual, a book of how-to's, and a set of video tapes illustrating the program . But in reality, we already have the "answer" to how to guide adolescents though the rite of passage inherent in being a Micro leader. I don't mean neat, tidy, scripted answers. Rather, I mean the answers will come as we learn to listen to our own voices, as we learn to become true to ourselves, as we learn to put to rest our own pasts, to live in the present, to stop fearing the future we can't control, and begin to hope in a future which is beyond our control. As we become these kinds of people, we will experience the answers that those whom we invite into this rite of passage, Micro leadership, will need from us.

The Classroom Transformation

What will we have when all is said and done by choosing and mentoring Micro leaders? A classroom where the Dance of the Dolphin is encouraged and practiced. Instead of a classroom that is only open to either Traditional dance steps, or Unconventional dance steps, which we saw contrasted in the Great Debate in Tables 1-1 and 1-2, we will have a classroom in which all students are free to participate in the Dance of the Dolphin and free to pursue what they will need to get their learning needs met. Instead of a classroom which is merely re-formed to be like school "the way we've always done it," or un-formed to leave children on their own in the hope they will find their own way to adulthood, we will have classrooms which are transformed: Classrooms that don't ignore or hide from problems, that don't scold children who point out problems, but which have the courage to admit to the problems and then to live with them in hope until new possibilities emerge as solutions. We will have classrooms in which student Micro leaders draw us adults and their fellow students along in the successful Dance of the Dolphin.

Reality Checks

1. Do you agree or disagree that most of the industrialized world operates in the order: Have, Do, Be? (First I decide what I want to have, then I set goals for what I must do to have that, then acquiring what I want makes me who I am—or at least influences it). Justify your answer.

2 What concerns do you have about delegating some of your authority to students? Discuss these with someone else who is also reading this book. After your discussion, play devil's advocate for each other: how could your concerns be overcome or safeguarded?

3. There is a proverb that says, *Today I'll study the children I meet. I'll learn much from their gentle beauty.* During school today (or with your own kids if you're at home), make a list of the things of gentle beauty you see because kids saw them first. The proverb goes on: *Anyone who keeps the ability to see beauty never grows old.*

4. Continue your list for 14, 21, or 30 days. At the end, reflect on what you've learned.

5. Use Figure 3-1 with one to three student leader candidates. After selecting the ones you feel are qualified, give them several small tasks to do for two weeks. Discuss with them at the end of that time how you and they feel about the experiment.

6. Explain how the Dance of the Dolphin can work between student leaders and followers—without adults involved.

Chapter Four

Inviting All Students to the Dance

In Chapter One, we were introduced to the Dance of the Dolphin. In Chapter Two, we explored some of the ways of being that teachers may want to explore in order to set the stage for the Dance. In Chapter Three, we took a look at how we might want to begin to put student leadership into place. Now, we will want to look at how to make the benefits of the Dance of the Dolphin available for all students; to invite all students to the Dance. In more practical terms, we will need to see how one might actually set up a Micro system in the classroom. But I would like to begin by reinforcing the reason we must do this, as introduced in those earlier chapters.

If we are to survive with our coterrestrials—better, if we are to allow them to survive, and even to thrive—it will take cooperation between us adult educators and kids, just as it did between man and dolphin. If the man had orchestrated everything, it would have been an entirely different event, more like that of a trainer and a "tamed" animal such as we might see in a circus or a zoo. In those places, the animals are merely performing as they have been trained to do. If we want children to emerge as healthy adults and not just to perform to please their trainer or the crowd, then they must be allowed the legitimacy of natural feelings, responses, and even failures, which lead to better focus, realistic expectations, and resiliency for future challenges. "[As spiritual people we] are invited ... to join our lives to a vine that is *power*, the opposite of *force*, and thus to experience our own released empowerment" (Wuellner 2001, 13). Just so, the Dance of the Dolphin invites us adults to exhibit the power of letting go, the opposite of force, so kids can experience their own released empowerment. There are five specific reasons why kids will need to be welcomed to the Dance, with us letting go, if we are to nurture their empowerment and so a healthy childhood, adolescence, and adulthood.

The first reason we must invite everyone to the Dance is all kids need to see the cause-and-effect relationship between what they do, the choices they make, and what happens in their lives. Teaching the need for considered choices, and the truth that their choices lead to certain outcomes, is cogently expressed by Conrath (2001, 586):

> When authorities babble on about personal responsibility to students who believe that their lives are controlled by external forces, they receive in reply blank stares or such helpless remarks as "It's not my fault; other kids were doing it too." "I wasn't skipping; I was home." "I wasn't late; the bell just rang before I got there." I'm not making up these responses. This is how these young people see the world. Things happen over which they believe they have no control. If schools do not take on the obligation to develop an authentic sense of responsibility in their students (as well as imposing external obedience when necessary, though the two are very different), the students will never acquire it.

The basis for this belief that external forces dominate their lives leads many of these societal *have nots*, those who may already be part of a marginalized group, to an alternative view of gaining success. Establishing Micro, however, gives them hope for accomplishing their goals in ways that will be beneficial for them and acceptable to society.

Second, the material participation of children in classroom decisions is far and away more supportive of democracy than the monarchy that has reigned in classrooms for hundreds of years, teacher talk and textbook assignments *about* democratic concepts notwithstanding. One way to teach such cause and effect is with the *experience* of democracy, versus merely giving an abstract explanation of the rationale for democracy. Do we want kids who can analyze our democracy but have no experience with, concern about, and passion for the messy process? Or do we want our kids to have experienced authentic democratic principles in action?

This point is made convincingly by Harvey (2001) as he talks about the lack of student motivation in learning science: "In some ways, the answer is embarrassingly simple: To increase science learning give students a reason to want to learn science" (p. 49). When we hear people disparage children for acting out, perhaps even criminally, we could draw a parallel. To increase student humanity and civility, give them a reason to want to act humanely and civilly. Having a say in how their day goes, with a voice that is taken seriously by others, can be that reason—and is one of the foundations of the Micro structure.

Third, there are several popular theories on the diversity of learning needs among students today. Of course, I am partial to my own view, the four learning perspectives[1] (Kennedy 2001b), but there are other good people who have suggested their own theories of learning differences. Some of the better known include multiple intelligences (Gardner 1983/1993); several takes on learning styles (Dunn 1996; Guild and Garger 1985; Entwistle 1988); temperaments (Kagan 1994; Keirsey and Bates 1984); personality types (Myers and Briggs-Myers 1980/1993); the eight areas of learning (Levine 2002); a triarchic view of intelligence (Sternberg 1985); an emphasis on emotional intelligence to balance the previously overwhelming emphasis on analytic thought (Damasio 1994; Goleman 1995); and brain-based learning (Kotulak 1997; Caine and Caine 1991; Sylwester 1995). Taken together, this body of work amounts to an emergence of overwhelming evidence of the existence of legitimate differences in learners. Consequently, we must see that any form of classroom management that favors—even demands—one type of learning environment to force students to learn in concert with just one type of teaching perspective or philosophy is inherently unrealistic and ineffective.

> There are differences in the ways that people prefer to behave, to think, to be and therefore to learn. These psychological preferences are not necessarily linked to ability. They're all equally valid and are more significant than we used to think.
>
> If we never have an opportunity to use our preferred styles of learning, we tend not to learn effectively.... (Scottish CCC 1996, 11)

Fourth, the fear of failure and of success, which we first mentioned in Chapter Three as being a danger to potential leaders, is true of all students.

> One destructive practice is that of rehearsing in our minds the outcome of a threat or problem, usually expecting the worst.... If we're going to rehearse anything, let it be an outcome that includes the best for everybody, including ourselves. (Mel B. 1996, May 17)

Many children have experienced an overwhelming sense of failure in their young lives (although much of that is not real, but only perceived, an outgrowth of one's sense of worth, which as we've discussed can be very damaged by the time a child reaches adolescence, and then further damaged *by* adolescence itself). Of the thousands of students I have had the privilege to know, I can think of only a handful who really had a good sense of their own worth. The fear of success is just the flip side of this issue: If I as an adolescent don't honestly believe in my worth as a person—not for what I've achieved, but just because I *am* a person—then how can I allow myself to believe I really deserve success? Or if I am successful (as judged by other people), why do I never feel like it's enough; why am I always striving for more? And since I probably believe I don't deserve this success, then I may believe it's a fluke, and I live in constant fear that the bubble could burst at any time.

Fifth, we must help students begin to see that life is not an all-or-nothing proposition; that one's life is not destroyed by one mistake or even a series of mistakes; that such mistakes do not define us. Yet as silly as it sounds when we put it this way, this is exactly how society sees things. We only have to think of how we love to categorize people to see that we tend to see people in all-or-nothing terms: He's an alcoholic; she's a druggie; that kid's a thug; that politician is dishonest. A more accurate appraisal might be that he has/had a problem with alcohol, but we all have *some* besetting weakness. She used to have a problem with drugs but had the courage to get help and is now recovering. Sure, that kid has been in trouble with the legal system, but none of us can change our pasts and he's trying hard to grow out of that life. That politician is not perfect and my hope is he will just come clean about this mistake, and that we can then admit politicians are human and that all people make mistakes.

> Properly viewed, all mistakes are for learning purposes. We often have to make a few mistakes before we can learn anything. Sometimes a mistake can occur simply to teach us one basic lesson—that we are human and cannot be perfect in everything we do. (Mel. B. 1996, April 18).

Establishing Micro: The Balance of Democracy

We grow as human beings when we admit and submit to compliance and conformity (e.g., laws of the land, laws of nature), when we admit our equality with others. At the same time, we want to remember that all of us are unique, and we deprive the universe of what only we can give it if we focus solely on our equality and sameness.

Translating this to the Dance of the Dolphin, with the aid of Figure 4-1 which continues and builds on its earlier forms, we are reminded that the "sameness" qualities are compliance and commitment, while the "uniqueness" qualities are commitment and community. The universe, the world, our cities and neighborhoods, our classrooms, and ultimately our students are incomplete without both sides, and all four steps of the Dance.

Getting Started: Preparing for the Beginners' Dance Class

There are several levels at which Micro can be practiced. And while you're obviously free to begin with an advanced form, unless you actually have some experienced dancers already, such a class can quickly prove overwhelming and discouraging. For this reason, I would like to offer some suggestions for first setting up a very basic Dance experience, and only then evolving into a more complex system. Micro will naturally self-evolve anyway, so nothing is lost by such a beginning.

There are three components for a Micro system, regardless of the level of complexity: its organizational structure, some type of "token" economy, and a set of expectations or rules for conduct. In the beginning, these can be quite simple. For example, the organizational structure could be nothing more than forming the class into groups or, as I prefer to call them, teams. Each team could be given the freedom and responsibility—as we know, the two sides necessary to balance democracy—to elect a leader/facilitator and perhaps co-leader/facilitator, who could then appoint remaining team members to various duties. Examples of such

Figure 4-1
Setting the Dance of the Dolphin in Motion in the Classroom

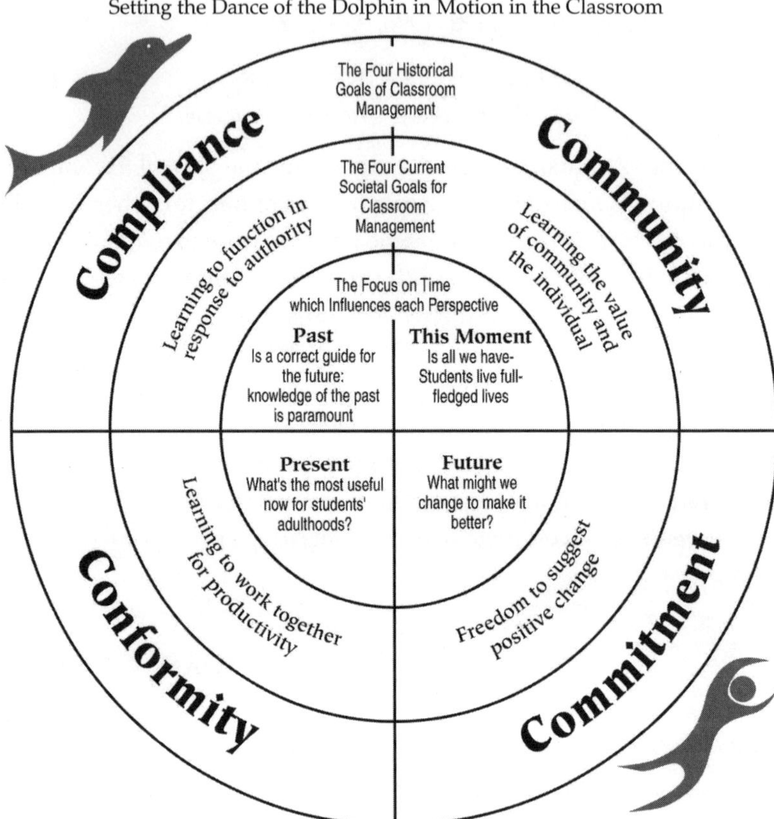

duties might include a group recorder for any team activities (such as brainstorming or problem solving); a resource specialist, for locating resources to help the team to learn; and an artist/communicator for drawing finished products and/or communicating with other teams when necessary. Of course, these jobs can change as needed, and as facilitators gain experience, they might be allowed to create their own team member jobs.

Teams could be responsible for such things as safety issues (as in science labs); staying on task during group work times; following class procedures and policies; basic cleanup (team work can be messy); peer tutoring (it's much less embarrassing to ask a teammate how to reduce fractions or what a word means than to have to ask the teacher and possibly widen the number of people watching); and sharing the strengths that each team member brings to the team.

Of course, in actuality, the duties that teams could take on are limited only by our—and their—imaginations.

The token economy can use any "currency" that is convenient for the teacher. Its value will come from what students are able to buy with it. It could be used for purchasing school supplies; renting a favorite seat (or even a special seat, as a bean bag or rocking chair) for a period of time; obtaining passes to special events such as a culminating movie or a school dance; or a "get out of homework for a day" card. The idea can be taken up a notch with a little planning, as by having a grab bag of small items, or less frequently, holding an auction for slightly more valuable items such as flashier pens or pencils, nicely bound journals, movie theater passes, paperback books, or whatever are the "in" things for kids at the moment. Local businesses will often be willing to contribute modest amounts of stock for such purposes.

This token currency is also very effective as a way to pay fines for breaking class/team protocol, procedures, or rules. It provides an intermediate step between doing too little, and doing too much by making the event overly formal, such as in having to hold a one-on-one conference with the student (very embarrassing for them, when they are probably already self-conscious about what they did), a parent or administrator conference, formal suspension, or perhaps even an SST meeting like the one we saw "for" Isaac in Chapter One. For example, I can fine a student a couple of Micro dollars for foul language—which they probably know is wrong and inappropriate for the place and time the moment they say it—and so actually make the learning experience humorous as they dig for their money, yet still effectively making the point.

The act of paying students can also be a teaching tool. For example, I may choose to pay them for their grades, teamwork, attendance, improvement over previous work, compliance/conformity/commitment/community, and so forth, and emphasize different things I—or Micro leaders—feel they need to be reminded of. I will want to be very careful over time to place value on all four dance steps, so that students will see the value in each of the different perspectives.

The set of expectations or code of conduct also presents a sterling teaching opportunity, but it is an opportunity that is easily missed. Most of us attended schools under traditional teachers for so long that we almost automatically jump to the old standby list of class rules: no gum or food, no talking out of turn, etc. To use such a list with Micro, however, is to miss a huge opportunity to turn the classroom from a place owned by the teacher, with students feeling like guests, to making it a place where students feel ownership and the accompanying freedoms and responsibilities. Ownership is the crux of whether one's class will actually begin to learn the Dance of the Dolphin or whether the dance will just be a failed experiment in the mind of the teacher.

The difference is not so much what goes on the list but in how the code is generated, or perhaps better, in *who* generates it. If the teacher has the code prepared before students ever enter the room, there is little incentive for student buy-in. The Dance of the Dolphin is a partnership; both swimmer and dolphin must participate if the dance is to be real.

The final component to making Micro work is communicating with parents. I have found parents to be overwhelmingly supportive of student-shared ownership, of learning to be responsible for the effects of their own decisions. They do like to be informed, however; for example, it can be problematic if a student complains to a parent who has no idea of Micro.

The Intermediate Dance Class

The intermediate class has the same components we've already discussed, but they are taken to a higher level of student freedom and responsibility. This means there is more risk required on the part of the teacher, but also greater possible reward.

Again, it is important to take it slow: Begin where you are comfortable and let the Micro interactions, the daily process dictate when and how you make adjustments. This is how any self-renewing system, such as we find in nature, works, anyway.[2] Nature's own output is used as new feedback. We know our planet is made up of organisms that interact with and are dependent upon each other. To use a well-known example, we have only to recall the lesson we enjoy teaching youngsters (and for me, especially urban youngsters, who are always surprised by it), that we humans exhale carbon dioxide, which plants need, and through the process of photosynthesis these plants in turn "exhale" oxygen, which we humans need. So you might consider the "waste" (exhalation) of each day with Micro as important for your reflection process—the "photosynthesis" of reflection on the day's results by you and even your Micro leaders—as necessary for renewal of the system for the next day, or week, or year.

I would like to introduce this level of the dance through several graphics which I use as handouts, and also have made into chart-sized laminated posters for my classroom. The handouts are combined for new students into an "orientation packet," which is reviewed with students in class, then taken home and reviewed with parents. An acknowledgment must then be returned to me, including both parent and student signatures. This packet consists of Figures 4-2 through 4-4.

The first item in the packet is a cover letter which I use to introduce and orient parents to the concepts of Micro. The student has already received such an introduction by Micro leaders upon enrolling in the class and has also had a day to see how the system works. She or he thus becomes not only the courier of the packet, but an ambassador to their parents for the effectiveness of, and usually the excitement for, the program. Communication is especially important with those parents who have experienced any sort of difficulties in dealing with schools before. "Tensions between schools and families have always been particularly strong for parents of children with disabilities" (Osher and Keenan 2001, 9), and, I might add, for parents and children who have had problems or philosophical differences with mainstream, comprehensive schools and are attracted to alternative forms of schooling, or at least the idea of new possibilities in the way we do things. No matter what is in your cover letter, just having one and inviting parent input is really important.

It seems logical to me that the next bit of information which students and parents will want to know, will be the organization, (see Figure 4-2). Please remember that this is the intermediate level chart, which would be appropriate for the intermediate dance class: students and teachers with some experience in Micro. Please note that I offer two alternatives: a government model, for the teacher/class which prefers to elect representatives (replicate a democratic model); and a corporate model, for the teacher/class which is often more popular with high schoolers, who often hold part-time jobs, or are looking for them.

Let me point out some aspects of the Micro chart. First, I always reserve for myself as the teacher (who is responsible to those outside the class for issues of safety, etc.) the position of governor or chairman of the board. This places me outside the workings of Micro, and so ensures that it is a true, working system—that vital, authentic interactions are truly taking place between students. As the outside authority, I also have the unquestioned authority, as governor, to impose martial law on those rare occasions when society truly breaks down, or, as chairman, to call a board of directors' meeting to make suggestions or get us back on track. Second, I like to assign each team the responsibility for being the champion for one of the Dance steps. This is so that when we get busy with the business of learning and things get messy, we don't leave anyone out.

I have seen Micro economics set up to be practiced in a variety of ways, as I have shared these concepts with preservice and inservice teachers over the years. You will notice from Figure 4-3 that the actual currency may be cash, stocks, checks, or time if a student doesn't budget well and runs out of Micro currency. Other ideas are points, debit cards that are issued with a certain value at the beginning of the week, say, and then punched for each purchase or fine. This seems especially popular with PE teachers, who in large comprehensive schools may have 250 students, 50 or more in each 50-minute block, every day. Adding another element to an already rushed situation may backfire, hence the cards that may even be maintained by the class leaders in the teacher's office.

Purchases, rentals, fines, and bonuses would follow along the lines of those things already described under the token economy in the beginner's class section. Of course, as the Micro organization becomes more comfortable with the system, student leaders and the teacher may think of ways to modify it so that it becomes even more effective. I believe anyone willing to try this concept will find that the framework is solid; the specifics are limited only by our own imaginations and experience.

The Micro code, as seen in Figure 4-4, is again only meant to be a beginning point for you. This just happens to be what is in use in my own class as I write this. By the time you read these words, however, it probably will have evolved substantially. But again, the specifics are for you and your students to decide—with the acceptance of your students' parents and administration. You may notice in the "Levels of Response" section that I have tried to include all four dance steps, so that we begin with

Figure 4-2. Micro Organization

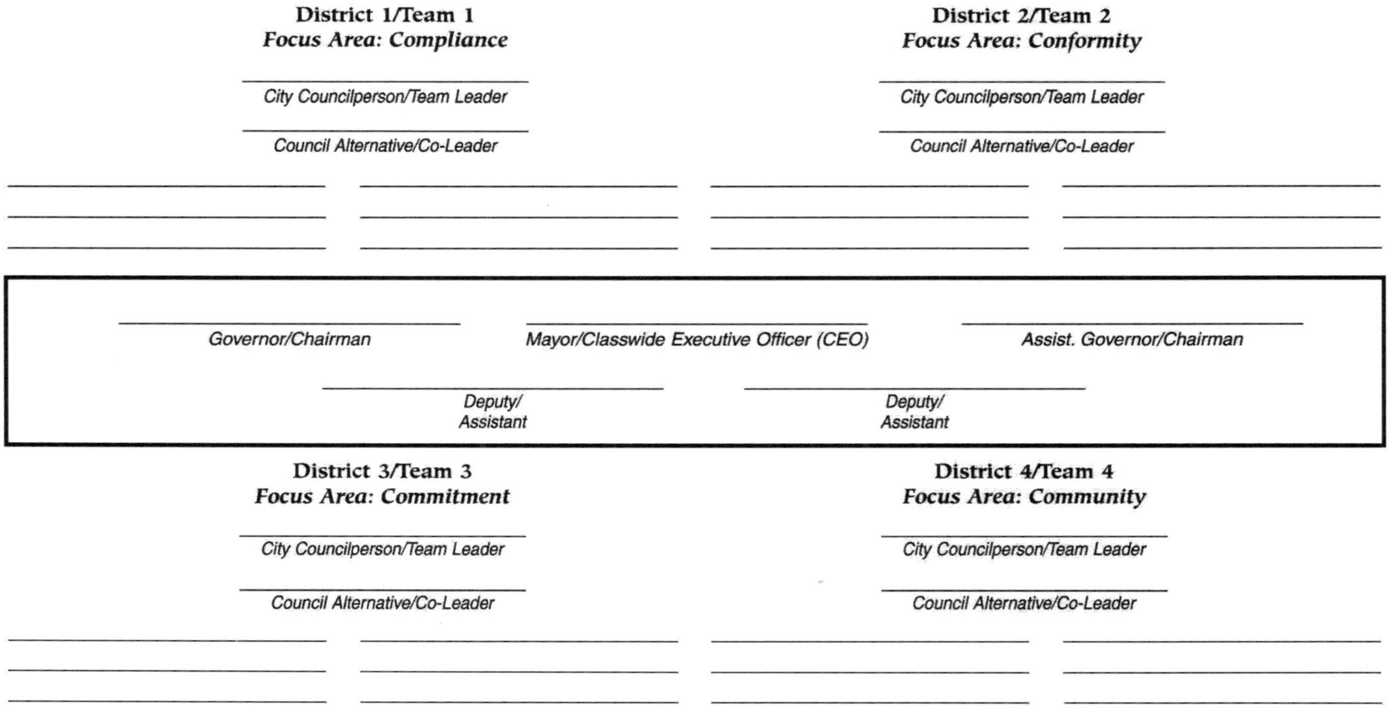

District 1/Team 1
Focus Area: Compliance

City Councilperson/Team Leader

Council Alternative/Co-Leader

District 2/Team 2
Focus Area: Conformity

City Councilperson/Team Leader

Council Alternative/Co-Leader

Governor/Chairman

Mayor/Classwide Executive Officer (CEO)

Assist. Governor/Chairman

Deputy/ Assistant

Deputy/ Assistant

District 3/Team 3
Focus Area: Commitment

City Councilperson/Team Leader

Council Alternative/Co-Leader

District 4/Team 4
Focus Area: Community

City Councilperson/Team Leader

Council Alternative/Co-Leader

Representatives/Leaders are responsible for their district's/team's focus area to the whole class.

Figure 4-3
Aspects of Micro Economics

1. Students are paid for the amount and quality of academic work completed each week.

2. Types of "currencies" that may be used: Micro dollars, Micro stocks, Micro checks, Time (e.g., extra work may be used as currency).

3. Sample expenses might include the purchase of school supplies; rental of school supplies; donuts (occasionally); any penalties levied on the MicroCorporation as a whole or on individual "employees."

4. Martial Law. When the privilege of Micro is abused, the Governor or Deputy Governor, or the Chairman of the Board, will impose martial law which may last for an hour to a week:

- No gum or food except at 15-minute lunch
- No talking
- Stay in seat except with permission
- No group assignments/work (to be made up later); individual academic work only
- Whole class fine to be paid with detention or voluntary cleanup duties

a reminder that the class is a place where the student has both freedom and responsibility, and that these must balance; that the student must be committed to herself and the class if it is to be a place where we can all be happy and fruitful. If the next level is required, you can see that it takes the form of a reminder that we are a community, and that people in a community share space, goals, needs, and respect.

Only after these reminders do we get into the traditional manner of dealing with infractions (Levels 3 and 4), which requires compliance and conformity. If there is widespread disregard for the freedom to operate in

Figure 4-4
Sample Micro Code of Conduct

Infractions	Levels of Response
Irresponsibility Class Misdemeanors. Responses start at Level 1.	1. **Reminder** of student's personal goals (Individual Learning Plan)
Improper language Dress code violations Contraband Tardiness, Truancy Not doing schoolwork Encroaching on class time Dereliction of duty Endangerment (minor) Repeatedly minor offenses	2. **Warning**. Written response (e.g., apology letter); Minor fine: (1 to 3 Micro dollars) 3. **Extra cleanup/Detention** (student's choice); Moderate fine: (4-5 Micro dollars) 4. **Substantial Fine** (10-15-25 Micro dollars on the individual, on the chief
Maliciousness Class Felonies. Responses start at Level 3.	5. **Martial Law: Loss of job or pay** for individual, team, whole class 6. **Outside Contact**: parent, principal, probation, police *and* dropped from the class or suspended with 20 days individual martial law upon return to class
Putdowns, gossip, rumors Bullying, hate crime Invasion of privacy Vandalism Destroying public property Fraud, cheating, theft Tampering with MicroCorporation Inciting trouble Disrespect of any adult	***All fines are doubled for District/ Team Leaders and tripled for Classwide Officers.***

harmony with responsible action, then I may have to call for martial law for a period of time—perhaps an hour, perhaps a day, or even longer. Although distasteful, I believe this is part of my job in order to underscore that my personal freedom must respect the personal freedom of those around me, which is shown through personal responsibility. I believe having this option in the real world *inside* our classroom follows closely the real world *outside* our classroom, which allows lessons to be *caught* by students even when such lessons aren't *taught* through overt lesson plans.

Be, Do, Have: A Sacred Space

Returning to a concept introduced in Chapter Two, if I can muster the courage to *be* in the moment, if I can nurture students to *do* their best because they have a renewed hope, then I *have* the possibility of creating a special place, a space made sacred because the whole becomes so much greater than its parts.

Again, the old Welch admonition said it well: *There are three things worth living/losing our lives for: truth, justice, and mercy.* Micro systemically incorporates all three. Why not try it?

Notes

1. My theory *does* have the distinction of being the only one I know that was developed by a classroom teacher, and tested, honed and ultimately proven in the crucible of the classroom. In this sense, my theory has been researched in perhaps the best possible manner, with student product being added back into the feedback loop, to become new input. See Chapter Six, "School Reform: Viability Through Feedback" in *Lessons from the Hawk* (Kennedy 2001b).

2. Again, see Chapter Six *Lessons from the Hawk* (Kennedy 2001b), where this concept of educational renewal as an open system is developed. In short, my hypothesis is that using student work (output) as feedback (renewed input) is the model for educational reform that we should be using, instead of all the top-down theory and research from those who never set foot in classrooms.

Chapter Five

Advanced Classroom Leadership

Learning in Micro

"Only those who will risk going too far can possibly find out how far one can go," T. S. Elliot told us. This chapter is for those willing to take the risk of going deeper than the versions of Micro in the previous chapter, in order to see how far this concept might take them and their students. The route I recommend will involve synthesizing different ways of learning, specifically the four learning perspectives, with the Micro organization.

Actually, a classroom led in this advanced manner sounds more complicated than it is. It may initially invoke images of yet more complex versions of my earlier graphics. In fact, however, only one of the three components of Micro, the organizational chart, even need be altered. The currency and policies/rules will work just fine as they are. In fact, even the organization chart could remain the same; it will just be infused with a new element: the self-understanding of each student of her or his own learning perspective and the need to actively contribute his or her uniqueness to Micro.

Specifically, we are looking for the contribution each student can make by understanding and appreciating their own dominant learning process. As you may be aware, the technical term for such understanding of one's own thinking is *metacognition*. While much of the literature on metacognition strikes me as needlessly complex and impractical for actual use with students, I believe the idea is valuable in the classroom-tested and pragmatic area of learning perspectives. It has been my experience that students' ownership of thinking about their own thinking can be very powerful, indeed (Kennedy 1994).

I think the reason that self-understanding of learning perspectives—especially for kids—is so central for me is captured by the psychiatrist, Gerald May. May introduces the concept of giving our *intentionality* room to breathe, as a means to rekindle passion and desire.

> Of all the things I dislike about psychiatry, I most abhor the notion of adjustment. What divine power ever said we should adjust ourselves to the ways of our world? Is our society (and its system of education) so perfect, so just, so loving that it is worth adapting ourselves to?... The choices we make—and therefore the way we feel about ourselves—are determined less by what we long for and more by what is controllable and acceptable to the world around us. After enough of this, we lose our passion. We forget who we are.... It is imperative, not just for our individual ... growth but for the hope of our world, that we begin to reverse this process. We need to expand the space between desire and control.... We must give our intention room to breathe. (1991, 46)

When I first sensed the spirit of May's message in my students—that is, the need for breathing room in order to be able to intentionally nurture every student's passion for their unique purposes—I began to look for ways to do this in the classroom. This began with evaluating and sometimes trying existing takes on differentiated learning—multiple intelligences, learning styles, and triarchic intelligence, for example—but I found that all were very difficult to actually implement, given the budget and support realities of a classroom teacher.

But just then serendipity seemed to strike when I attended a workshop by Robert Garmston on presenting to adults. While many of Dr. Garmston's ideas were very good, one was particularly compelling for me, namely, that all adult workshop attendees had one primary question about any new material being presented. He represented these questions as beginning with one of four interrogatives: *What? Why? What if?* and *So what?* For ease of understanding, he further identified each of these four views with a symbolic profession: Professor, Scientist, Inventor, and Friend (Garmston and Wellman 1992). You may recall from earlier graphics (for example, Table 1-1 and Figure 1-2) that I have come to use Garmston and Wellman's symbols interchangeably with my own: the Professor as either Professor or Academic; the Scientist as Trouble-shooter or Investigator; the Inventor as Inventor or Innovator; and the Friend as Guide or Communicator. The longer I work with these concepts and use these titles with kids and adults, the more I appreciate having the flexibility of these interchangeable names. At differing times, a synonymous symbol may prove invaluable in further circumscribing each concept.

At any rate, Garmston's workshop proved to be one of those giant *Aha!* experiences for me. I knew immediately that I had to try these ideas with kids. To make a long story short, this process continued over a period of several years and proved to work for kids—and adults—beyond my wildest dreams. The curriculum planning and instructional processes that emerged from these trials, which allowed me to reach all four of these learning perspectives, are the subject of my first book, *Lessons from the Hawk* (Kennedy 2001a). Along with the story of the solidification of the four perspectives, *The Hawk* gives detailed curriculum planning processes and classroom-ready charts that will ensure reaching all four of the perspectives in every class. There is even a chapter devoted to homework that will stretch students from their natural perspective, or roots, to their least comfortable outlook, or wings, synthesizing the whole process with Bloom's taxonomy in the bargain.

So then, understanding one's *own* learning perspective and how others might differ, is extremely important. We discussed some of the advantages earlier. You may remember that in the Introduction we saw some *So What?*-outlook student Communicators able to resolve a potentially dangerous situation. And in Chapter One, we saw Isaac-the-Communicator bewildered at the demands of his Professor- and Investigator-perspective teachers. Even if a student finds herself stuck with a teacher who is ignorant of and/or obstinate about the reality of learning differences, that student's metacognitive awareness of her own learning perspective and needs can offer substantial protection against failure in such a teacher's class.

Learning Perspectives and Micro

Students' understanding and use of learning perspectives is a powerful and empowering tool, and it is key if we are going to truly educate children in humane and democratic ways and principles. At the same time, we have already seen that Micro is also powerful. Perhaps it should be no surprise, then, that using them together is synergistic—and can become almost magical. It creates an atmosphere that is often wished for, and sometimes promised in more commercially promoted programs, but in my experience, this atmosphere is rarely achieved by anything invented by non-teachers. The benefits I'm talking about are not only doable, but also free to any teacher or school willing to acknowledge the legitimacy of differentiated learning needs, while also allowing for variations in classroom management needs such as we've seen with the dolphin dance steps. These two components will naturally work together, a confluence of student self-understanding with a totally supportive classroom environment. But if this is truly realistic, *how* do we do it? The answer is, through the third level, or the advanced Dance of the Dolphin.

This advanced dance will require several new components if we are to carry it off: a solid background for ourselves; an instrument for helping each student identify her or his own learning perspective; ways to further help these students understand what this means for them (to interact with the ideas); and teaching them how learning perspectives and Micro can support each other by assigning each student to a team with one of the four perspectives as its ongoing responsibility and focus. Let's take up each of these parts in turn.

In Figure 5-1, we might recognize some of the material from Table 1-1 configured in the format of JoJo and Dean's dance. Working from the outside in, we first encounter the interrogatives. These remain perhaps the handiest way for me as a classroom teacher to keep track of each student's perspective, to communicate with each student, and the easiest metacognitory reminder to them. It is also a reminder to me of how to phrase inquiries I assign so that each student's interest will be piqued, jump starting each one's perspective.

Moving inward, we see a more technical descriptor for each perspective. The desire to know *What?* goes naturally with the pursuit of analytic understanding—an ability to make sense of fragments of a whole

Figure 5-1
Recognizing the Four Learning Perspectives
Traditionalism (Teacher is the Authority, Students Learn Best from Parts to Whole)
Unconventionalism (Teacher is a Colleague, Students Learn Best from Whole to Parts)

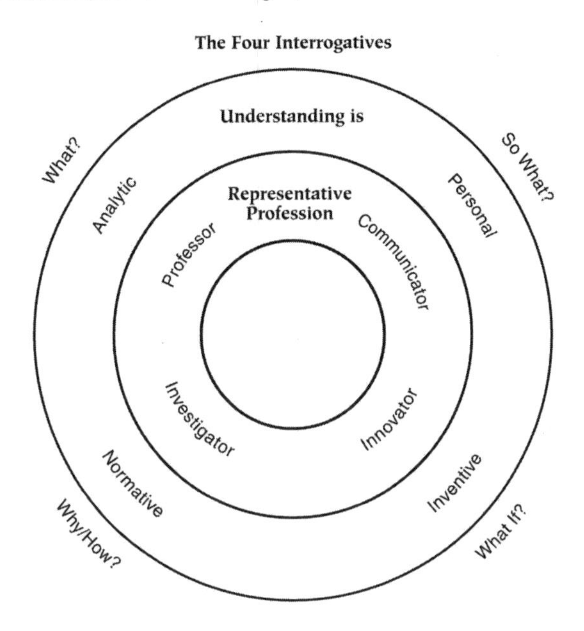

(such as abstracted facts like dates, names, and vocabulary lists). As we move on, we see that those with this learning perspective are the symbolic Professors, as alluded to in Chapter One. In *Lessons from the Hawk* I illustrated each of these symbols with three or four famous people. For example, Plato, W. E. B. Du Bois, Confucius, and Hypatia are offered as examples of Professors. The point of these examples is to offer students concrete examples of successful people throughout history who have shared their outlook. As you can see by visiting the Web (see inset at right), I even ask each student to learn something about one of these exemplars from their learning perspective and to turn in a report detailing what they have discovered. They receive a certificate of congratulations, which is also a summary of their outlook for future reference.

Learners of the other Traditional perspective, those who focus on the *why* and *how* new information and/or new or broken things work, could be seen as pursuing a norm. I call this a search for normative understanding. If my car is broken or my body is sick, these Investigators want to know why it's not working and how to return it to normal. Again, there

More on the Web!

For more on these student assignments, along with student certificates to be awarded upon their completion, please visit the Dolphin website at <http://www.great-ideas.org/DolphinMaterials.htm>.

For your convenience, the adult version, the LSOS, is also posted on the Website. For a more detailed explanation of the LSOS, and its implications for curriculum and instruction, you may want to refer to *Lessons from the Hawk.*

are many famous examples, from which I have chosen Abigail Adams, Maimonedes, Benjamin Banneker, and Aristotle.

Those learners who first ask *what if* when presented with a new idea or problem, are inventive in perspective. Presented with the same sick car or person as the Investigator above, instead of searching for normative solutions, these natural Innovators will begin to search for novel alternatives. To those of other perspectives, some of the ideas generated will seem ridiculous, while others may seem brilliant. We have only to think of the life of Einstein for a concrete example, although I also like to mention the lives and work of Martin Luther King, Jr., Su Song, and Margaret Meade.

So what learners are those with an Unconventional learning perspective, and you might recall that we came to see Isaac in Chapter One as viewing the educational enterprise from this outlook. For these people, learning begins with the personal relevance of the academic material, the significance it has to people, especially those they know or feel empathy towards. This personal perspective is not tolerated well in our task-driven, annually scripted (content and performance standards) educational atmosphere. Because those with this perspective have been shunned by the educational establishment consistently for at least the past century, I would like to spend just a little extra time with this group.

When I call these learners Communicators, I don't mean the affected, slick, Madison Avenue style of "communication," which in my lifetime has become a popular college-degree major: always having the right answer, always making the sale, always convincing the other side I am right. Rather, by commune-icator I mean the person who quite naturally exchanges meaning with others; who is in tune with others' verbal *and* non-verbal "language"; who lives easily in like-minded community, who is aware of (communing with) her or his surroundings, including the whole (or holistic) environment; who sees nothing peculiar about collegiality, whatever their position on the power scale.

Tilden Edwards (1995, 97) enlightens us about the spiritual foundation of such commune-ication:

> Authentic spiritual life ... has always held together the love of God, self and neighbor.... You shall love your neighbor as yourself.... The Hebrew scripture behind that last verse ... can be translated as "love your neighbor as *the being of* yourself.

A close friend shared with me her insight that "neighbor" in this sense includes all that we should/can love, including nature, which is intertwined with our existence. This extrusion of Edward's view would seem to meld with the Buddhist idea of "codependent origination (everything that exists does so dependently on other things)" (Audi 1999, 105). The well-known Zen master, Thich Nhat Hanh (1991, 39), puts this perspective into simple terms:

> After a retreat in Southern California, an artist asked me, "What is the way to look at a flower so that I can make the most of it for my art?" I said, "If you look in that way, you cannot be in touch with the flower. Abandon all your projects so you can be with the flower with no intention of exploiting it or getting something from it." The same artist told me, "When I am with a friend, I want to profit from him or her." Of course we can profit from a friend, but a friend is more than a source of profit. Just to be with a friend, without thinking to ask for his or her support, help, or advice, is an art.
>
> [It is better if] we stop, and we look deeply. We stop just to be there, to be with ourselves and with the world. When we are capable of stopping, we begin to see and, if we can see, we understand. Peace and happiness are the fruit of this process. We should master the art of stopping in order to really be with our friend and with the flower.

So the commune-icator is one who most naturally is able to stop, who is aware she lives in co-existence with everything around her. We might take a moment and think how different this is from a traditional teacher-directed, teacher-talk, task-driven classroom environment.

Harriet Tubman was this type of communicator. Just the knowledge that she packed a pistol to discourage her underground railroad charges from changing their minds, thereby endangering all the others, communicated well enough her intent, without a word being spoken. César Chávez always seemed to me to eloquently communicate his position through his humble, understated manner, whether or not he chose to use words. Mother Teresa was also one to "speak" through her actions, preferring to work with people than to talk about it. Mahatma Gandhi, just as Mother Teresa, often used words sparingly. For me, Gandhi's famous aphorism stands as admonition and summary: "Be the change you wish for the world" (Prakash 2002). A wholly other communicator, on the other hand, who didn't mind talking about the problems he saw with the formality of society in his day, was Søren Kierkegaard. He would not, however, engage in an analytic, professorial discourse. Rather, he preferred to indirectly "direct" others to come to understand for themselves the importance of actions matching words.

Now that we have taken a brief look at each of the four learning perspectives, we educators might be better equipped to help students begin to understand their own perspective. But how will we identify each of their perspectives? Given enough time, every teacher familiar with these concepts could probably identify each student in an authentic manner, that is, through observation of the student. But probably more often we will want to begin to work with a student's strength right away. To expedite this, I have developed the Student Self-Observation Survey, or SSOS. A few sample prompts, along with samples from the LSOS, which first appeared in *Lessons from the Hawk*, are offered here. Both surveys are available online at <www.great-ideas.org/DolphinMaterials.htm>.

Synthesizing Learning Perspectives with Classroom Management

As we begin the final synthesis of learning perspectives and classroom management, we might first realize the presuppositions that different people will bring to the learning enterprise. That is, we must ask,

Sample Student Self-Observation Survey (SSOS) Protocols <www.great-ideas.org/DolphinMaterials.htm>

4. I believe that			
the most commonsense way is the right way.	*any* way that I can get something to work is OK with me.	there's always one *right* way that we should look for and follow.	there is often a *better* way that I can usually find with time.
9. When taking any test, it is important to me that			
I have the time and freedom to use my own ideas and scenarios.	test questions should allow me to explore the *how* and the *why*, not just facts.	I be allowed to work with others, just as in the real world.	there are clear, black and white, right and wrong answers.
10. School authorities			
should always be open to changing the policies.	usually know best; they are in charge for a reason.	should be watched to make sure they do the right thing.	should find the way of doing things that works best.
15. I like classroom talk that			
is mostly the teacher supervising students working together.	leaves me time to freely think up my own ideas on the subject.	is mostly the teacher — who knows the most, anyway.	is mostly the students — who often work just fine without a teacher.

Sample Learning Self-Observation Survey (LSOS) Protocols (Adult Version) <www.great-ideas.org/DolphinMaterials.htm>

9. I usually like to do a difficult task			
in a group of equals (without necessarily having a formal leader).	it varies, but anyone I work with must want to find out why and how we got the answer.	alone or leading a group.	alone or with a motivated partner.
10. In learning a new skill or taking a new subject, I believe that			
the personal relevance of the subject and its basics must be learned simultaneously.	I have to master the basics before going on to the advanced stuff.	I must understand how the basics work but may need to look at the overall picture to do that.	the basics will take care of themselves if the subject is meaningful to me.
11. I like to			
usually work before I play or relax.	*always* have fun first and do the work afterward.	*always* get my work done first, and *then* play or relax.	*sometimes* work first, but other times play first and save the work for later.
12. I most like			
traditional or customary things.	questions or puzzles that I know will have an answer.	the same kinds of things my friends like.	inventing things: stories, ideas, or gadgets, for example.

what are the various goals of education which different camps have held? We must be scrupulous in digging out all the views we can so that the final synthesis can be as close to a consensus as we can make it.

While I don't wish to seem to speak for anyone else, I do believe we can once again use certain categories to represent the main currents in the historical expectations people have held for schools. And once again, it seems the number of these categories keeps coming up as four.

The four functions of the comprehensive high school historically could probably be agreed to as the desire for intellectual, social, vocational, and personal development (Chapman 2000; Education Week 2000). While we could spend quite a bit of time just demonstrating the veracity of this statement, I think we can fairly say these four categories are representative of the 20th century development that resulted in the phenomenon which we call "high school." We can also call upon our earlier work in this book, remembering in Chapter One the two sides and four distinctive categories of the Great Debate: Perennialism, Essentialism, Progressivism, and Personalism.

Team Assignments and Grading

Team Assignments

The only thing left in turning the advanced form of classroom management into reality is to take all the concepts discussed to this point and use them to generate a new Micro corporation organization chart. A sample appears on the web at <www.great-ideas.org/DolphinMaterials.htm>. Setting up this organization is fairly straightforward.

After identifying each student's learning perspective, the Micro leaders and I discuss which team the student may most benefit from and contribute to. We may try a direct match of the student's perspective with the team's focus, e.g., a Professor on the Academic-minded team. Or if, say, the Creative or Communal team needs a bit more focus, we may assign them a new-to-our-class Professor. As another example, if the Technical team needs some fresh ideas, we may add an Innovator or a Communicator to the mix. If even that doesn't boost the team's ability to contribute to the entire class, we may even find a more seasoned person of Unconventional perspective and make them that team's *leader*. But however it is done, once all students are assigned to a team, we can begin to nurture the focus of each team to be responsible for making sure that the entire class looks at the material at hand from the team's perspective, whatever it may be.

Team Grading

I almost always hear the objection when introducing this material to preservice and inservice teachers that the trouble they have experienced with groups is that some students will do most of the work, while others do very little or none. How then to grade fairly? It's quite simple, really. I give a grade (points) to the entire group. It is up to the group to decide on a fair distribution of these points. Inherent in my conception of fairness is that a consensus is reached, that a shy but hard-working student is not short-changed; that there is no subtle bullying; and that everyone then signs off on the result by initialing next to their points. I have found this extremely effective. Again, a sample worksheet for you to download and use or improve can be found on the web at <www.great-ideas.org/DolphinMaterials.htm>.

Advanced Classroom Leadership

While the advanced Dance of the Dolphin, blended with the sweep of the Hawk, is perhaps not a good place to begin to implement the ideas in this book, it is far more doable than one might think. And while one is beginning with a less complex version of Micro, the synergy of learning perspectives and student-empowered classroom leadership can remain a destination on the horizon, where sea meets sky.

Reality Checks

1. Take the LSOS <www.great-ideas.org/DolphinMaterials.htm>. Do you believe the results accurately identify your primary learning perspective? Why or why not?
2. Summarize the concept of learning perspectives. Guess the perspectives of two or three children you know (from your classroom, school, family, or neighborhood).
3. Explain how Hawk and Dolphin meet on the horizon, that is, the advanced Dance of the Dolphin.
4. Sketch a graphic representation of the advanced Dance of the Dolphin.

Chapter Six

Dancing in the Street

We began this journey by looking at the actions of some kids who had been positively influenced by the Dance of the Dolphin. It seems fitting to end our journey in the same manner, with a look at a few more of these kids. Since I work in a class that is the last resort for adolescents who have not found success in other settings, sometimes my illustrations may seem somewhat dramatic. But, as we said earlier, if Micro works with these kids, it will probably only be better with those who have less antipathy toward school.

Many of these "throwaway" kids—which is how society treats them—have become renewed under Micro. They experience a new interest in school, a new willingness to comply and conform to the demands of society at large, and often find a direction for their lives that is more authentic for them than the standard fare they have received in traditional schools. For many, Micro becomes a rite of passage through adolescence and into young adulthood—and perhaps often a much more hopeful outlook.

And as we said, this rite of passage accomplishes naturally and authentically most of the things the educational establishment has abstracted into separate "programs" such as service learning, community service, anger management, bullying prevention, violence prevention, and drug and alcohol abuse prevention.

Instead of requiring one or more of these splinter programs in an effort to promote the learning of citizenship, Micro is holistic (as is life, but perhaps more critically so in any democratic society); it integrates the entire school experience of the youngsters involved. I have found that many of these students have learned to find their own personal, significant, unique life rhythm because they were invited to the Dance of the

Dolphin. And because their own needs are met, they are able to take the Dance with them when they leave the class. In a sense, we could say they learn to move the Dance of the Dolphin from the classroom to the larger society: that they have learned to dance in the street.

If I were asked to pinpoint which elements compose the heart of the success of kids who had passed through Micro and taken it into the world with them, I would probably say this "heart" is composed of four outflow valves. That is, kids learn the benefits of living *now*, and how living now is enhanced by *giving*, through *humor*, and by living in the *light*. But instead of abstracting these arteries, or components, let's just watch for them as they unfold in the following anecdotes about students.

David

David was a kid whose SOS results identified him as a Professor. I'm always a little surprised to see one of these traditional learners end up in my alt-ed classroom. By all accounts, David should have done well in a traditional comprehensive high school setting, where the preponderance of teaching was traditional and academic. So each one of these students is a good reminder to me that there is more to school success than just one's learning perspective. In fact, traditional learners are always something of a challenge for me, since my own learning perspective is more on the unconventional side. I've learned to deal with this, but this mix still sometimes throws me. But back to David.

Being a Professor, David was very organized, diligent in his schoolwork, a task-oriented person, and also not afraid of hard work. He was also very responsible. And I trusted him immediately, which is not always the way I feel about gang-involved kids. I should point out that I don't hold gang membership against anyone; I separate the person from the gang, as long as they reciprocate by leaving the gang outside the school, which most do when they see how Micro can work for them. In fact, in some neighborhoods, belonging to a gang is almost literally the only way a kid can avoid getting beaten up every time he walks out his door. Going along to get along takes on a whole new meaning—quite literally, a life saving one.

Another reason some kids turn to gangs is that they have no functioning family to speak of, and gangs are equally accepting of all—beautiful and not so beautiful, smart and not so smart, popular and outcast. They become a life-support system which many kids don't have at "home." David was such a kid. His father and mother were both alcoholics, his mother then dying of cirrhosis of the liver. I never saw his father sober, and that includes the times he dropped David off at 7:30 in the morning (only once or twice in two years).

David learned in his time in our class to leave the past in the past, to live in the present, to laugh a lot, and that doing these things while having school success, allowed him the freedom to dream the future. He found he no longer needed to dull the pain of feeling not enough by using drugs and fighting. He grew into a young man I would have been proud to call my own. While still my class CEO, David began to work at a restaurant chain, and quickly began to be promoted. While he did not complete high school on time, by the age of nineteen he was third-tier management. Will he stay at that company and make a career of it? Probably not. How many of us do? But he has experienced success in something he wanted to do—and he knows he can go someplace else and do it over again. Living a day at a time in Micro, giving daily to those who needed help when he served as CEO, laughing and causing others—including me—to laugh and thereby giving us the gift of healing, living in the light, without having to feel he must keep secret his past, his family life, or in any way to feel guilt for leaving the past in the past. Doing the Dance of the Dolphin, I believe, changed David's life.

EVELYN

Evelyn the Investigator brought a "major" perspective in conformity to the Dance of the Dolphin, to Micro, and a "minor" outlook in community. So, I learned to meet this seventh grade mayor's demand for conformity of the class—and me!—with a certain collegiality, with a willingness to be a part of the conformity she believed in so strongly. I would treat her ideas about which activities and logistics the class needed with acceptance, but also with gentle reminders that we needed to give everyone a voice, that we needed to be a community to all perspectives equally well.

On the other hand, she would sometimes go a little overboard on the "community" dance step, and I would remind her that there were some school policies and procedures that we needed to heed. Even though this occurred before the standards mania, we did have district and state guidelines to consider, and so couldn't just take off in any direction we wanted. She always took these reminders in good grace, and I watched her grow in both her academic abilities and her leadership skills. She actually organized the major portion of a culminating activity, which involved five classes going into the community to conduct a survey of the public on some real-world city council plans. The findings were later presented to our local city council by these students. The whole enterprise was followed on camera, and a professional video was produced to encourage other middle school students to become involved in local government (Institute in Local Government 1994). The tape and accompanying text, which Evelyn also helped work on, are still available.

Evelyn entered my class designated an English Language Learner, even though her English was better than mine—and her Spanish, of course, put me to shame. Because of this she sometimes butted up against what I consider institutionalized racism, and so she and I fought a few running battles with those who thought an ELL kid deserved fewer library privileges, and couldn't possibly be qualified for gifted or talented programs (although this was never said outright). We fought hard, but we still lost most of those battles. However, we may have won the war. Today, Evelyn is the president of her university's chapter of a social activist group, as well as in the honors program. She is finishing her degree and preparing to teach elementary school, even though she could write her own ticket to more "sexy" careers and could probably earn ten times as much as she will as a teacher.

JAMES

James the Innovator brought his natural enthusiasm and his commitment to this new idea called Micro that I had introduced to his 4th/5th grade combination class that I was assigned one summer when I was still teaching middle school in an elementary district. I hadn't ever taught elementary school to speak of, and so had no idea how this group would take to the whole idea of Micro. Well, James took to it—ran away with it, really. His commitment made the whole thing work, and all I had to do was dance the complementary step of complying to his expectations for me—and to ask the rest of the class to do the same, once I had explained James's reasoning, and how it would help us.

The unspoken bargain was that his commitment was based in part on his desire to be the mayor, and that if he won, I would support him wholeheartedly. Of course, he still had to campaign against the others who wanted to be mayor, and he had to win. He set about his campaign with exuberance, commitment, and style, which together were enough to convince a majority to vote for him. And the rest, as they say, is history.

James "made" that whole summer experience for me, but much more importantly, for the other kids as well. On visitation day at the end of the summer, we had parents (and even school board members) make comments like: My child has never been so enthusiastic about school; I have never seen a program like this before—we need more like it (school board); and, Could you be my son's teacher in the fall—this is the first time he's wanted to come to school (of course, I couldn't, which was heartbreaking for all of us). But these rave reviews were not really about me. They were about James, and the community he and his peers had built by doing the Dance of the Dolphin.

James and I found out later that we lived just around the corner from each other, so I had the opportunity to watch him process through the years; to sort of keep informal tabs on him. I could see he did well all through middle school and high school, participating in afterschool activities instead of the more popular street scene. Today, he is close to graduating from college, and says he wants to make a difference in politics. I would stake everything on the fact he has turned out OK, that even though a member of a high-risk minority group, he won't become another statistic.

JOSIE

Josie the Communicator was the first—and only—Ladino student I remember teaching. I learned a lot from our interchanges. She was bright, witty, and unabashedly inclusive in her approach to others and life in general. Josie exhibited the common communicator characteristic of understanding others—including me—before we could get the words out. This intuitive understanding meant that she would know things about the general class dynamic almost as it was forming or changing, and certainly long before I caught on. This served her well as CEO, in that she could build community (when she wanted to—after all, she *was* still an adolescent) like none of the other learning perspectives.

Like David, Josie was the child of parents with their own substance abuse problems and this made her life difficult. Getting rides to school from someone sober, getting basic needs met, such as health care, food in the house, and clothes to wear as she outgrew the old ones, were common problems. Still, Josie persevered until she was ready to return to the comprehensive high school. She is still there, on target to graduate with her class.

Josie challenged me to meet her community-building step with a willingness on my part to comply in a collegial manner, so that the entire class might benefit. Of course, I sometimes would have to set limits to the collegiality, while at other times I would have to go beyond my previous comfort zone in becoming more collegial for a time. The Dance of the Dolphin challenged both Josie and me to stretch and grow, and we and the entire class were better off for it.

Conclusion

Does Micro resolve every student problem? No. But then does the larger democratic society resolve every problem for all of us? Of course not. Still, it's probably the closest we can come in a type of government that will give us a chance to resolve our own needs and problems. In the same way, Micro is the absolute best we can do for kids during the six to eight hours a day they are with us. It means a willingness to do the complementary dance steps with them, thus honoring their needs, their brightness, their unique giftedness. It means modeling and encouraging their living now, giving now, seeing the humor in things, and living in the light.

There's a restroom at my favorite Starbuck's where the light is operated by a motion sensor. But the sensor level is often set to be much too sensitive. If one is in the restroom and motionless for about three seconds, the light goes out and it becomes pitch dark. When this first happened to me, I thought how scary that would be if a child happened to be the occupant. Anyway, since I can't get in and out of the restroom in under three seconds (and definitely not since I passed 40!), I find myself almost dancing in order to keep the light on. But I realized one day that that might be a good thing. Because it became a reminder that unless I'm always dancing in another important room—my classroom—leading the Dance of the Dolphin, the learning environment can instantly and without warning become pitch dark. And that's scary for children.

References

Anonymous. 1976. *Alcoholics anonymous*, 3rd ed. New York: Alcoholics Anonymous World Services.

Bai, H. 2001. Challenge for education: Learning to value the world intrinsically. *Encounter: Education for Meaning and Social Justice* 14(1): 2-16.

Barlow, J. 1999, July 23. Bringing quality into the schools. *The Houston Chronicle*.

Biehler, R., and J. Snowman. 1990. *Psychology applied to teaching*, 6th ed. Boston: Houghton Mifflin.

Brandt, R. 2001. No best way: The case for differentiated schooling. *Kappan* 82(2):153-156.

Briggs-Myers, I., and P. Myers. 1995. *Gifts differing: Understanding personality development type*. Palo Alto, CA: Consulting Psychologists Press.

Buckingham, M., and C. Coffman. 1999. *First, break all the rules: What the world's greatest managers do differently*. New York: Simon & Schuster.

Cahill, T. 2000. *Dolphins*. Washington, DC: National Geographic Society.

Caine, R., and G. Caine. *Making connections: Teaching the human brain*. Alexandria, VA: Association for Supervision of Curriculum and Instruction.

Canter, L., and M. Canter. 1976. *Assertive discipline: A take-charge approach for today's educator*. Santa Monica, CA: Lee Canter & Associates.

Chapman University. 2000-2001. *Graduate Catalog*. Orange, CA: Author.

Conrath, J. 2001. Changing the odds for young people: next steps for alternative education. *Kappan* 82(8): 585-587.

Cummins, J. 1985. *Empowering minority students*. Sacramento, CA: California Association for Bilingual Education.

The Dalai Lama, and H. Cutler. 1998. *The art of happiness: A handbook for living*. New York: Riverhead.

Damasio, A. 1994. *Descartes' error: Emotion, reason, and the human brain.* Alexandria, VA: ASCD.

Dewey, J. 1963. *Experience and education.* New York: Collier. Originally published 1938.

Diamond, M., and J. Hopson. 1998. *Magic trees of the mind: How to nurture your child's intelligence, creativity, and healthy emotions from birth through adolescence.* Penguin.

Dickinson, D. 2001, Fall. *Revisiting Maslow.* New Horizons Electronic Online Journal.

Dunn, R. 1996. *How to implement and supervise a learning style program.* Alexandria, VA: ASCD.

Drucker, P. 1993. *The effective executive.* New York: HarperCollins. Originally published 1966.

Eckert, R. 1996. Guidelines for creating effective rites of passage. In *Crossroads: The quest for contemporary rites of passage.* Chicago: Open Court.

Education Week. 2000. *Lessons of a century: A nation's schools come of age.* Bethesda, MD: Editorial Projects in Education.

Educational Leadership. 2001, September. *Making standards work.*

Edwards, T. 1995. *Living in the presence: Spiritual exercises to open your life to the awareness of God.* HarperSanFrancisco.

Elkind, D. 1995. *Ties that stress: The new family imbalance.* Cambridge, MA: Harvard University Press.

Elkind, D. 1995. The death of child nature: Education in the postmodern world.*Kappan* 79(3): 241-245.

Entwistle, N. 1988. *Styles of learning and teaching: An integrated outline of educational psychology.* London: Fulton.

Erickson, E. 1968. *Identity: Youth and crisis.* New York: Norton.

Fried, R. 2001. Passionate learners and the challenge of schooling. *Kappan* 83 (2): 124-136.

Furr, D. 2001. Leave no child behind: We may be institutionalizing the very cycle of failure we seek to break. *Education Week* 20(9): 34-36.

Gardner, H. 1993. *Frames of mind: The theory of multiple intelligences.* New York: Basic Books. Originally published 1983.

Garmston, R., and B. Wellman. 1992. *How to make presentations that teach and transform.* Alexandria, VA: ASCD.

Glickman, C. 2001. Dichotomizing education: No one wins and America loses. *Kappan* 82(2):147-152.

Goleman, D. 1995. *Emotional intelligence: Why it can matter more than IQ*. New York: Bantam.

Gonzalez-Balado, J. 1996. *Mother Teresa: In my own words*. New York: Gramercy Books.

Guild, P., and S. Garger. 1985. *Marching to different drummers*. Alexandria, VA: ASCD.

Hakuta, K. 2001. *Key policy milestones and directions in the education of English language learners*. Washington, DC: Rockefeller Foundation Symposium.

Hallahan, D., and J. Kauffman. 1994. *Exceptional children: Introduction to special education*, 6th ed. Needham Heights, MA: Allyn & Bacon.

Hanh, T. 1991. *Peace is every step*. New York: Bantam.

Hazelden Information and Educational Services. 1989. *Keep it simple*. Center City, MN: Author.

Heschel, A. 2001. *I asked for wonder: A spiritual anthology*. Edited with introduction by S. Dresner. New York: Crossroad.

Hirsch, E. (ed.). 1996. *What your kindergartner needs to know: Preparing your child for a lifetime of learning*. New York: Dell.

Howard, C. 1995. *Dolphin chronicles*. New York: Bantam.

Institute in Local Self Government. 1994. *Participating in local government*. Video Sacramento, CA: Center for Youth Citizenship.

Kagan, J. 1994. *Galen's prophecy: Temperament in human nature*. New York: Basic Books.

Keirsey, D., and M. Bates. 1984. *Please understand me: Character and temperament types*. Del Mar, CA: Prometheus Books.

Kennedy, M. 1994. The ownership project: An experiment in student equity. *Social Studies Review* 33 (2): 24-30.

Kennedy, M. 1996a. A teacher's manifesto: Designing learning which cures rather than causes academic risk: Part 1. *Journal of At-Risk Issues* 2 (2): 3-15.

Kennedy, M. 1996b. A teacher's manifesto: Designing learning which cures rather than causes academic risk: Part 2. *Journal of At-Risk Issues* 2 (2): 16-27.

Kennedy, M. 1999, Spring. Elephants and adolescents. *Journal of Court, Community, and Alternative Schools* pp. 13-15.

Kennedy, M. 2000. Building the bridge to hope with the four Ws of learning and life. *Reaching Today's Youth: The Community Circle of Caring Journal* 4(4): 51-55.

Kennedy, M. 2001a. *Lessons from the hawk*. Brandon, VT: Holistic Education Press.

Kennedy, M. 2001b. Reversing the Cycle of Despair. *Reaching Today's Youth: The Community Circle of Caring Journal* 5(2): 10-15.

Kennedy, M. 2001c, Fall. Managing the active, differentiated-learning classroom. *New Horizons For Learning Electronic Online Journal.*

Kennedy, M. 2001d, Summer. Today, I'd probably just drop out. *Paths of Learning* 9: 6-9.

Kennedy, M. 2001e. Where do we go from here? September 11 and jury duty. *National Coalition of Alternative and Community Schools.*

Kohn, A. 1996. *Beyond discipline: From compliance to community*. Alexandria, VA: ASCD.

Kohn, A. 2000. *The case against standardized testing: Raising the scores, ruining the schools.* Portsmouth, NH: Heinemann.

Kotulak, R. 1997. *Inside the brain: Revolutionary discoveries of how the mind works*. Kansas City, MO: McMeel.

Kozol, J. 1991. *Savage inequalities: Children in America's schools*. New York: HarperCollins.

Krashen, S. 1985. *Inquiries and insights: Second language teaching, immersions and bilingual education, literacy*. Englewood Cliffs, NJ: Alemany Press.

Lerner, H. 1989. *The dance of intimacy: A woman's guide to courageous acts of change in key relationships*. New York: Harper & Row.

Levine, M. 2002. *A mind at a time*. New York: Simon & Schuster.

Mahdi, L., N. Christopher, N., and M. Meade (Eds.). 1996. *Crossroads: The quest for contemporary rites of passage*. Chicago: Open Court.

Matthews, C. 1999. *The Celtic spirit: Daily meditations for the turning year.* San Francisco: HarperSanFrancisco.

May, G. 1988. *Addiction and grace*. San Francisco: HarperSanFrancisco.

May, G. 1991. *The awakened heart*. San Francisco: HarperSanFrancisco.

Mel B. 1996. *Walk in dry places*. Center City, MN: Hazelden Information and Educational Services.

Mercogliano, C. 1998. *Making it up as we go along: The story of the Albany Free School*. Portsmouth, NH: Heinemann.

Miller, R. 1997. *What are schools for? Holistic education in American culture* (3rd rev. ed.). Brandon, VT: Holistic Education Press.

Miller, R. 2001. Making connections to the world: Some thoughts on holistic curriculum. *Encounter: Education for Meaning and Social Justice* 14 (1): 29-35.

Mogabgab, J. 2001. Editor's Introduction, The vineyard issue. *Weavings* 16(5): 2-3

Mother Teresa. *No greater love*, edited by B. Beneate and J. Durepos. 1989. Novato, CA: New World Library.

Nation, C., and L. Stevenson. 2001, Spring. Balance of power: Making sure youths are seen *and* heard. *Reaching Today's Youth.*

Nerburn, K. 1999. *Make me an instrument of your peace: Living in the spirit of the Prayer of Saint Francis*. San Francisco: HarperSanFrancisco.

New Horizons for Learning. 2001 September. *The Building Tool Room: Democratic Classrooms.*

Ohanian, S. 2001. *Caught in the middle: Nonstandard kids and a killing curriculum*. Portsmouth, NH: Heinemann.

Osher, D., and S. Keenan. 2001, Spring. From polarization to partnership: Learning to listen to families. *Reaching Today's Youth* 5 (3): 9-15.

Prakash, M. 2002, Summer. Gandhi's truth: Be the change you wish for the world. *Encounter: Education for Meaning and Social Justice* 15(2): 3-5.

Prystowsky, R. 2002, Winter. Honoring others in the moment, or, Loving without regard to outcome. *Paths of Learning* 11: 3-5.

Ravitch, D. 2000. *Left back: A century of failed school reforms*. New York: Simon & Schuster.

Reys, R. 2001. Curricular controversy in the math wars: A battle without winners. *Kappan* 83(3): 255-258.

Ruiz, D. 1997. *The four agreements: A Toltec wisdom book.* San Rafael, CA: Amber-Allen.

Sayers, D. 1987. *The mind of the maker.* San Francisco: HarperCollins. Originally published 1941.

Scottish Consultative Council on the Curriculum. 1996. *Teaching for effective learning.* Dundee, Scotland: Author.

Sleeter, C. 1996. *Multicultural education as social activism.* Albany: State University of New York Press.

Steel, S. 1988. *The content of our character: A new vision of race in America.* New York: HarperPerennial.

Sternberg, R. 1985. *Beyond IQ: A triarchic theory of human intelligence.* New York: Cambridge University Press.

Sylwester, R. 1995. *A celebration of neurons: An educator's guide to the brain.* Tucson: Zephyr Press.

Watson, R., and B. Brown. 2001. *The most effective organization in the U.S.: Leadership secrets of the Salvation Army.* New York: Crown Business.

Wuellner, M. 2001. The power of the vine. *Weavings* 16(5): 12-15.

Young, A. 2001 Mandalas: Circling the square in education. *Encounter: Education for Meaning and Social Justice* 14(3): 25-33.

Zona, G. 1994. *The soul would have no rainbow if the eye had no tears: And other Native American proverbs.* New York: Touchstone.

About the Author

MARK KENNEDY lived several "lives" before coming to education. In the early 1970s, he served a four-year enlistment in the Vietnam era U.S. Navy. This was followed by an undergraduate degree in German, Latin, and history from California State University, Fullerton, and then graduate work in Greek language, theology, and medieval European studies. The 1980s, however, found him cash poor and so he took a position in the financial services industry, specifically in securities, insurance, and small business financing. After experiencing both high finance and low finance, Kennedy found his way in 1990 to his real calling, teaching, eventually earning a Master of Education degree from the University of La Verne.

KENNEDY is currently an alternative education teacher in San Bernardino County, California, and an adjunct professor at Chapman University, Ontario Academic Center. He has also served as an acting principal, lead teacher, mentor teacher, master teacher, chair and visiting team member for many self-study and strategic planning focus groups and action teams, and is a CTA statewide trainer of trainers in Gang Awareness and Self-Esteem. Kennedy was selected as the 2001 Teacher of the year for Social Studies by the Inland Empire Council and the 2002-2003 Alternative Education Teacher of the Year by the San Bernardino County Superintendent of Schools. This is his second book.